Opcit at Large

Also by John Barr

The War Zone

Natural Wonders

The Dial Painters

Centennial Suite

The Hundred Fathom Curve

Grace

The Hundred Fathom Curve: New & Collected Poems

The Adventures of Ibn Opcit

Book Two

Opcit at Large

John Barr

Red Hen Press | *Pasadena, CA*

Opcit at Large: The Adventures of Ibn Opcit, Book Two

Book design and layout by David Rose

ISBN 978-1-59709-259-3 (tradepaper)
ISBN 978-1-59709-240-1 (clothbound)
Library of Congress Cataloging-in-Publication Data
Barr, John, 1943–
Opcit at Large : The Adventures of Ibn Opcit, Book Two / John Barr.—First Edition.
pages cm
I. Title.
PS3552.A731837O63 2013
811'.54—dc23
2012045710

The Los Angeles County Arts Commission, the National Endowment for the Arts, the Los Angeles Department of Cultural Affairs, the City of Pasadena Cultural Affairs Division, Dwight Stuart Youth Fund, and Sony Pictures Entertainment partially support Red Hen Press.

First Edition
Published by Red Hen Press
www.redhen.org

Acknowledgments

Grace was first published as a book in 1999 by Story Line Press. The author wishes to thank the book's editors and readers. A stage version of *The Adventures of Ibn Opcit* was performed in 2008 at Victory Gardens Theater in Chicago. The author wishes to thank Bernie Sahlins.

Contents

The Afterdammit

Opcit en Afrique

The Last Cosmonaut
A Christmas Tale

The Afterdammit

Scene 1. Burnt Offerings

Lightning reveals two souls, naked on a naked branch. They are recognizable but not as if alive, not like birds but like birds in the oven.

Num. Tumma Numma Tumma.

Soul 1

Lightning! How it bridles the air.
Seethes and scuttles like a centipede.
Under its repeated bites, this place—
Lord Bejeezus of the Alchemies, where am I?
Can this be Baja California?

Soul 2 (*A cough, as from the grave. The second soul, in a state of considerable dishevelment.*)

The doors are closing. Please hold on for dear life.
I haven't felt this bad . . . what day is tonight?
My head feels like a cantaloupe. A hailstone.

Soul 1

Those baked salt flats, like a pan of cookies
forgotten in the oven. What *is* this place?

Soul 2

I am so glad to see Camp Berkshire is back on the map.

Soul 1

Maybe it's the wrong Creation.
Maybe this is a flawed, discarded prototype.

Soul 2

Maybe God made this world, but lost it at dice.

Soul 1

Or perhaps He did not *create* the universe—
that was another god. And He was brought in later
to *inspirit* it.

Soul 2

Maybe *earth* was Purgatory
and they just didn't tell us. Would that make this Hell?

Soul 1

What if there *is* a judgment and an afterlife,
but we had it backwards? That would explain
why no good deed goes unpunished.

Soul 2

Just what we need, another ten theories
of the universe at rest. How did you get here?

Soul 1

For me the gateway was a king-sized bed.
A certain lady, avid to do the silly slant,
invited me in for a round of polar bipod.
She had just asked me, "How big *is* your shatska?"
when in walked the man of the house with a sushi knife.
One quick stroke and he held Leviticus aloft;
like a mad postmaster he canceled everything in sight.
I awoke on a conveyor belt with dirt, grass, dead animals . . .
"So *this* is where the dead go," was my thought.
And death for you was . . . ?

Soul 2

. . . like being sneezed on by an elephant.
You know how Manhattan buses lumber up Madison,
down unimpressed Fifth, asserting their asphalt rights?
Stepping off the curb I looked right instead
of left and was ironed by a thirteen-ton Express.
The canonical black I wore was mistaken
by the driver for the entrance to an underpass.

Soul 1 (*Looking him over.*)
I can see that. But who are *you*?
What are you, a null or a void?

Soul 2
How I look
and how I feel may be different things today.
This is as much fun as waiting for luggage.

Soul 1
Or watching dental surgery on TV.
Did you live the life you wanted to live?

Soul 2
I can't remember. But I think it was intemperate.

(Upon that word one of the shapes circling on thermals far above drops like a plummet to where the two souls sit.)

Demon
EEEEIIIIOOOOUUUU!

Soul 2
Healthy Jesus, what is that?

Soul 1
Another lightning bolt. But this one in slow motion.

Soul 2
More like the flaming horricide of an airliner crashing.

Soul 1
It floats like a parachute to ground.

Soul 2
It walks with a gnarly overblow . . .

Soul 1

like a spider . . .

Soul 2

. . . or as if drunkenness were God's ordinance.

Demon

Now *here* is a coy assemblage. Wing and wing
you occupy that branch, a couple of birds
looking for a place to bluster, a couple of roasters
on a hymnal tree. Truly you are two
for the specimen collection. *Look* at me!
I say you both are easy work for teeth.
Assjammer! Bring the flesh fork, the one for spitted meats.
We'll turn these till they make the spittle music,
till they let out a meaty warble. *Headlicker!*
No more animal hams of uncertain origin
for lunch. Here are your meat pies.

Soul 2

Divine Ordnance, have you come for *us*?

Demon

I came because I heard the magic word.

Soul 1

You mean "dental surgery"?

Demon

I mean "*intemperate.*"

Soul 2

I feared that. I feared you would say, "Your souls are mine."

Demon

Why would I say that? Why own souls?
You think we are dulotic here? Think this is some

slavish meat market? Some Grand Central of souls?
Or maybe you think mactation is our game,
and you are appetizers for the gods.
Enough of this Bonehead-and-Bonhomie routine!
Demons like me must have the personality
of a barber, able to get along with anyone
whose hair needs cutting—even if it's Tweedle Dum
and Tweedle Dee. We're here to *colloquize*.
You to learn, me to teach. You may ask me
anything—in the subservient sedate, of course.

SOUL 2

Blithe Spirit, where are we?

DEMON

You're on the hardscrabble of a narrow defile.
Below you stretch the Hemorrhoidal Plains.

SOUL 2

But what *is* this place?

DEMON

Welcome to La Paz, where mañana starts right now!
Welcome to the Awful Raffle. Welcome
to the living Hell!

SOUL 1

That lightning. It's like Kansas,
the way it crisps the plains.

DEMON

This isn't Kansas, Toto.
Each time it strikes—*One* one thousand, *Two* one thousand—
a soul enters or exits. It's rare to see
so many standing down. There must be a war on.
But the weather here is not about the frugality
of drought, the prodigality of blizzards.

That rainbow, for example, is the oxidizing
boundary between hope and despair.
This valley with its soda burn connects
to the hot parts of the planet. All this became,
with the advent of the human spirit, necessary.

SOUL 1

And what are those shapes, black like flapping crows?

DEMON

That one, goggle-eyed as a mantis, is Skiplash.
He loves his game of Double-Chase Whipping Boy
played to the strains of "Orpheus Come Home."
Over there, that's Ape Man with the scare of teeth.
(A connoisseur, he eats only the nugget of the heart.)
And Golgotha, breathing like a furnace.
They're playing the game we call Magma Sledding.
(For lunch they had one of those melted squirters,
one of those whaddeyacallem . . . Aldermen.
Ape Man said, "He makes my pee smell like sulfur."
And Golgotha, "That's better than asparagus.")
Are you *sweating*? Are we at your personal dew point?

SOUL 2

I'm just wearing my water on the outside.
May I perspire freely?

SOUL 1

And who, Great Shape, are you?

DEMON

It's the Demiurge of Deadpan! The Demon of Resolve
in the Domicile of Dommage! Flying by night
I soar the coarse winds of insanity,
the skies of leaden squalor, the nether now.
Descending like a *deus ex machina* in reverse,
I am the arch catastrophe of the lives you've led.

Soul 1

You seem to preside over a diminished empire.
You are a null perhaps, or a void? Admit it now,
you're one of those liaisons that has no history.

Demon

Or perhaps one of the 14,000 perimeters?
Actually, I'm not sure. I think of *me* as made
out of the raw material of adumbrage.
That is how I think of *you*. It seems that everything
is to some extent alert and to some extent inert.
As man to monkey, goblin to gargoyle: these vary
but by degrees of animus. Thus the "living rock."
Thus the "wooden-headed fool." You, as men,
I find to be highly imperfect. As clay toys,
you are devilishly clever.

Soul 1

Well I for one will not
sit here, fear enfolded in the pod of my body.
Oh sure, you give the *appearance* of reality,
but perhaps you're a figment of our febrile minds.
Maybe you're a Nobody listening to nobodies.

Demon

You're as diplomatic as a Mexican garbage truck.
As full and unabridged.

Soul 1

Don't be stupid scary.
How, for example, could you not know everything?

Demon

I don't know, why do all the medical students
in low-budget horror movies wear dirty lab coats
and look like hell? What a preposterous soul you are!
Is our knowledge perfect? No! It's more like watching the world

around the corners of buildings, reflected in a dental mirror.
Here you people are described as window units.
But we have our sources. I read the obits.
As your dog smelled you in life to know where you've been,
I smell you in death to know what happens next.
Mine is the foreknowledge of the first parenthesis.

Soul 2

Great Shape, is man made out of matter or spirit?

Demon

Out of webs of straw, bales of bone. One head
but two hands. Fairly long legs, and feet
like complicated metaphors for travel.
Slightly hairy, but hardly fur-bearing.
His ragged interior is like a planet's—all flum and guano,
crag and heat. But peopled by the airy crew—
the hungers to live, the appetites by which they do.
What's a man? An averaging and defying machine,
grounded and hysterical at times,
at times humorless and prehensile.

Soul 2

Is man, then, no different than other animals?

Demon

Octopus, leech . . . each member of the kingdom pertains
to a human type. My suckers get sore just thinking about it.
And man for his part pertains to other kinds.
The spider with its deplorable eyesight,
the wizened toad, rats—especially the rodents
and other mammals of inferior form.

Soul 1

But *are* we dead and is this Hell?

Demon

Ah, those are questions for all answers.
You have from the ancients this major misconstruance:
Hell as a place where souls hide out, each with a face
like a bloody stump, while we demons walk
the perimeter of the midrestone, choosing
with the care and precision of a feeding frenzy
which of you shall load the cross-hairs of our rotisserie.
Hell as that place which satisfies the need for justice;
as odious and grismal, in its way, as perfection.
(We had Dante here a while ago. Was he surprised!)
But these distortions invite contrivance. As if He
who threw the Devil here in the first place were then to command:
"Pitch the telephone marketers to the Eighth!"
No, Hell is something they got famously wrong,
an assault on the middle on behalf of the ends.

"Hell" here has little to do with punishment;
it has everything to do with consequence.
In the enormous simultaneous equation of existence,
Hell is that place where process comes to rest.
Hell is where we put the souls on hold.
The afterlife, or the afterdammit as we call it,
is a place where the passion goes out of passion,
where awareness for a bit can rise to contemplation,
even to a broad, spatulate inquiry
into the nature of things. Here in the quiet backwaters
of the Universe, informed by a knowledge
of the consequences of how you lived, but spared
the passions that put you here, you can reflect a little
on how you wish to redirect your soul-selves
the next time round. In this way we take Heaven
and tilt it sideways—

Soul 1

(So much for the Proclaimed Brightness.)

Demon

Perhaps you would prefer the Christian version:
Old men, crawled out from the ass-ends of their graves,
dropping their headstones on the freeway in their frantic
search for the great rubber-handled doors of Heaven?
Plato had it close to right, much good it did him:
He gave the soul a say in its next abide.
Do you know, by the way, what Socrates said,
when he arrived, to three-headed Cerberus?
"I won't need an attack dog, thank you. I married one."
Actually our complete layout here
was captured by one Gongol Horrificon,
an utterly obscure *philosophe*
of the 18th *siècle*. His Theory of Animadvertancy
slumbers on a shelf in an alcove of the Vatican.
Gongol's Law: A soul is a way of siting energy in space.
Gongol's Second Law: Space is a dimension of time.
And Gongol's Lay: You swivet awhile and then you die.

Soul 1

But what of us? Why are *we* here?

Demon

Let's simplify a little. Don't you know, a soul
is a set of passions projected through a great deal of time?
The spirit enters matter from time to time as the needle
of the seamstress enters and reenters the fabric.
(In like manner we of the apposite world are matter
that from time to time enters the world of spirit.
I myself was a gargoyle on the parapets of Notre Dame.
I was permitted into animate life,
I think, because I weathered well.)

Soul 1

So life
is not an affliction from which matter tries
constantly to cure itself . . .

Demon

nor a nightmare
from which it tries constantly to shake itself.
But values, to continue, are what the soul solves for,
what is grafted on, life by life.
One of the lyric poets, in their little throngs,
asked "What is a man but his passion?" "A man
is his passion informed by his values," was my reply.

Soul 1

You keep the poets here?

Demon

Over there,
in that locker next to "Lost Gunnery Sergeants,"
the one before "Tap Dancers, Tapestries, Taps."

Soul 2

And the soul, like a virus, survives by its ability
to mutate for the better?

Demon

Not exactly.
More like a solution in the early stages
of crystallization, trying to realize
the design implicit in its nature.
The soul projects a view of itself through time.
I think of a human being as a hologram,
a shimmering "if" projected by the soul.
Values are extemporized, attempted, attained . . .

Soul 2

. . . and life by life that form reveals itself
at a continuing rate of divulgence?

Demon

More or less.
I think of the progress of the soul

as like a flywheel in its nest of gears:
the shifting is a reaching out for its next of kin.
Do you notice how you both burn with the blue filigree
of a started fire, the founding kindling's flame?
Do you notice, when you speak, how your assholes
flutter and chirp in sympathy? Like bagpipes
you are instruments not yet done evolving.

Soul 1
(I thought it was an interminable flute solo.)

Soul 2
Then character determines fate?

Demon
From your ass to my ears.

Soul 1
But if character determines fate,
then predestination is not a divine decision.
It's a working out, in human terms, to a certain end.

Soul 2
As lime on a football field seeks the perfect line—

Demon
More like, drawing a curve, you must find the way
it wants to go. Have you noticed, the thing about a road
is the way it curves the same way every day?
So with a given soul.

Soul 2
But where does it lead?

Demon
Like any road, to a different place than where you are.
You hold some hope that progress is inevitable?

That everyone arrives at last at some golden mean,
a life lived with the proportions of the Parthenon?
No such luck. The hundreds of lives you live,
the wave after wave of feeling This One May Be Right,
do lead you some day to matriculate
to the state of where it is you really want to go.
That *could* be a conquest of indulgence, a happy potential
for coping with opportunity or peril.
Or it could be you will join the landscape, a chunk of limestock,
never to vote again.

SOUL 1

In which case
we'll take your place on the parapets of Notre Dame.

DEMON

You should be so lucky.

SOUL 2

Do we live forever?

DEMON

As it is in the nature of books to be used but not
consumed, so with your souls. Think of a library
the only thing on whose shelves are biographies
of your former lives. So you come to me,
your life one volume from a shelf of shapes.

SOUL 1

I have a problem with the arithmetic. The world
now numbers . . . seven billion souls? That's up
from one Adam, one Eve. Does this mean
the celestial ectoplasm increases, or is it
a finite amount stretched out among the bodies,
as you would add water to soup to make it go further?
And a follow-up: Are there places
from which we never come back to earth?
What happens to souls who don't reenter the clay?

Demon

You do have a rat-maze for a mind.
As to the difficult arithmetic that reconciles
soul-counts in reincarnation, know this.
There is a stillness near the moon,
a ground not happy nor hunting, but holding. There,
in the shatter of moonglow, souls by the foregone million mass.
In their intense unhappiness not to be of the earth—
denied epiphany by any of the four elements—
they send lightning, they eat holes in the ozone,
they buffet the earth with earthquake.

Soul 2

What is to become of *us*?

Demon

On this conversation much of that depends.
You sit here with the energy of a form released.
It is that rare moment when a man is defined
not by circumstance but by himself alone.
Athwart the fixed conveyance of his past,
he can become as great, as gracious or grotesque
as he is able. It is a moment of *self*-delineation.

Soul 2

A match, uncoupled from existence as an ordinary
thing, flares in the moment of its nova.

Soul 1

What is *your* role in what becomes of us?

Demon

I am here to restore the thoughtful part of you.
When men, unvalved by death, say good-bye
to the blood bustle in their veins, and the exaltations
of their bodies cease, they come to us.
They gather, no surprise, with the enthusiasm

of clams assembling for a clambake. (*You* came to us
like a couple of Mexican hostile beans.) Then life,
by which I mean matter that is aware
and is trying to do something about it,
generally seeks a renewal of innocence.
The gods make man as man makes bread—from a dough
that wants to rise. But like any of us you are
a bundle of exceptions looking for exemptions.
I am, like a horseman on a horse,
a Guiding Intelligence to your lack thereof.
I try to reduce the accidentalness of choices.
In a process not unlike collimation
we align your souls so that what comes next
will help make sense of who you really are.

As a first step we turn your appetites into something
you no longer live to enjoy. The soul,
deep in its chosen hold but seared from its desires,
can then reflect a bit before the redirection.

SOUL 2

The songness of the flesh . . .

SOUL 1

without the song.

DEMON

Which is why we have these little fireside chats.
I'm not here to make things hard, but we try to look at you
critically: Not only how good you are, but how good you aren't.
We could, of course, show you the harrowing highlights of your life.
But the masters here enjoy the subtlety of indirection.
There is no definitive damnation here. In this part of Hell
we spend a lot of time trying to help our clients
to perfect their understanding of their selves. Our interest
is in the creative uses of death and oblivion.
All we ask is that you be true to yourselves. Recognizing,
of course, that this is your chance to change that self.

SOUL 2

Why have we been placed together here?

DEMON

One shoe waits for the other. As the row
of upper teeth and that of the lower get to know
each other through years of chewing, we paired you two:
Alone, you're mere upended sharpness, together
you make a bite. Then too we thought
you two, like dogs, might well observe
the time-honored tradition of eating each other's vomit.

SOUL 2

Am I not entitled to vomit pink phlegm if I want to?

SOUL 1

Is there any possibility we could have a different demon?

DEMON

What's that, Serape Face? You could have Ornery Henri.
When a man forgets his potential as a beast of burden,
Henri helps him to recover that. He believes
adversity makes you equal to more things.
Or you could have Loblolly, who does things to you
with a rubber hose that cause his audience
to dissolve in laughter. And his newfound fell:
Allowing your gums to reaffirm their grip on teeth
before he unseats them again with a baseball bat.
Or we could simply leave you to enliven
the saliva dumps. But why not me?
I was as underemployed as a musical dwarf
waiting around for Christmas. Besides I do best
with souls having a failed sense of humor.
Did you know, by the way, that the banjo
was invented in Mexico?

SOUL 2

No.

DEMON

Actually
that's a total lie. But it would be *nice* for this moment
in the conversation if it had been.

SOUL 1

A sense of humor as infectious as rust.

DEMON

And as unforgiving as a telephone number
in its need to be exact. Did you hear
about the woman who showed up for her eighth abortion?
"Aren't you capable of a sustained relationship?"
her doctor asks. "Not with a fetus," she replies.
Ah, there is no business like this show business.
What do you do with a trail of *non sequiturs*?
Not follow them, of course! This will be
as sprightly and whimsical as a law colloquium.

SOUL 2

But it isn't fair! It's like telling
a couple of hamsters in a cage to "Get a Life."

DEMON

You have a problem with that, Tinder Head?

SOUL 2

I have no opinions, and no attitude problem.
Only a shorted light socket for a spine.

Scene 2. Weight Watchers

Demon

Now everybody say Hi, everybody say Hello.
And let the games begin. Let's play Twenty Questions.

Soul 2

All right. Animal, vegetable or mineral?

Demon

No, that is what we are here to determine;
it is to one of those states you are headed *for.*
This game is to find out where you came *from.*
In the last life whom do you suppose you were?

Soul 2

But I can't. I can't remember who I am. Or was.

Demon

Think carefully. We have the time.
Lost souls are not lost spoons. And finding them,
like the slow regeneration of kidney stones, takes time.
I'll give you a clue. In life you had a hulking bulk
and a perfect memory for the bottom.

Soul 2

A whale!

Demon

No, although the nation of the manatee,
when you do a float roll, greets you as its own.
Another clue: In life you wore a monk suit
for the sink-or-swim.

Soul 2

A churchman?

Demon

Close!

In life you were a large man with a florid calendar.
You were known, among many things,
as the Enormous Bo-Diddly Man.

Soul 2

Much in the way of bells it does not ring.

Demon (*Mimics.*)

Does dis sound familiar?
The thing about the past
is how little trace it leave of itself. And humans,
not so much as a fern print on Wyomingonian shale.
Aren't we, finally, who our fellows say we are?

Soul 2

Opcit!

Demon

We have a winner! And in life you were . . .

Combe

Apotheosis Combe. In matters of Church I was
inspector of the people's spirit. As head prelate
I gave my flock, charged with the indecision of prayer,
the Pompous Encyclical. Mine was the metaphysics
of the pounded pulpit. I catered to the Dukes,
to their invented notions of finery.

Demon

(A savage *Hissonery;* a savage *Yerhonory.*)

Combe

I was a man of ectoplasmic integrity,
a jack of all ministerial trades.

Demon

You were one of the dominant squanders of your time.
When Combe in his great preponderance arrove,
when he entered the nave ahead of that momentous butt,
the congregation hastened to move aside.
("There is that priest," they whisper, "who sitting can encompass
toilet seats complete.")

Combe

If the cheeks of my hams
can parlez-vous a toilet seat, what's that to you?I lived in the care of
the fatting effects of food,
but mine was not the body pinched thin by smoking.
Who are dieters, after all, to live like wizened stalks?
To bring to my responsibilities a kind
of corpuscular abundance, to err at times
on the side of inundation: This I found
not inappropriate. I gained a few surmounted pounds.
And then a few.

Demon

With contingent metabolisms
you grew great. In your furious penchant for food,
able to condense it at alarming rates
into disheveled pounds—

Combe

Not so, not so.
Like Jacob with his angel, I wrestled my stomach
to the ground and mastered it. Yes, indeed.
All things in moderation. I ate a moderation
of *potato* chips, drank a moderation
of white *wine*, a moderation of raspberry *piddle* . . .

Demon

. . . of chocolate-covered *strawberries*,
of any immersive *bub* of fat or fruit.

No stranger to the *grab* of cheddar, the *hanker* of garlic
in a meatloaf sandwich, you had your eye
on the entire licorice production of North America.

COMBE
I was eating my way to health!

DEMON
Rotundly overweight you kept eating,
and if anything ate more. A dignitary of dross,
you exhibited a kind of slovenly rectitude.
Towards the end your sermons got pretty bad.
"This is the pot in which you are allowed to pee."
Or "Give thanks that you live in a world that elicits
the Holy Cow response." So did your prayers.
"The Lord is my putative Shepherd." Or "Our Father,
whatever art thou, whichever be thy Name."

COMBE
I remember one sermon, "The Taking of Christ's Walk"—

DEMON
You may not denigrate the Dauphin.
That is one thing you may not do here.
But I remember. You told your laity, "Give thanks
for buttons, without which our shirts would blouse
and our pants fall down." Like a toilet whose handle
needs that extra jiggle, you ran on and on.
At the end you displayed a punditry of beefsteaks.
You were prone to frequent the Religious Bakery.
Your body was willed to science to give them a last,
awestruck look—along with your books, *Other People's Food*
and *The Exploded Gourmet.*

COMBE
Did I have other lives?

Demon

Head of the Burdock Mission. Founded 1862,
"Established for religious, charitable and educational
purposes, and for the extraction of precious metals."

Combe

I was the Archbishop McAndreypoop!

Demon

You dealt in the unctuous twaddle of the Saved,
you stole from the Subsidy for the Sisters of Collusion.

Combe

Oh, I remember. Privately they called me
Guacamole Man. And before that?

Demon

Recluse Demortia, in the service of
the Avalon of Requisite Confierto,
himself a fleshly Italian potentate.

Combe

He was so good he could blow corn out his nose.
That fatal fall down stairs, it caused me to blow a kidney.
And then?

Demon

Pinochet Emolument,
a pope so long incumbent his minions forgot how to make
the elective smoke blow black or white . . .

Combe

How I sweated and frankincensed for that!

Demon

. . . hence the phrase, "as squeamish as papal smoke."

COMBE

Before that?

DEMON

Publico Phlebitis, a noble
of Roman nose; then Oxyruncus, a Roman of noble nose.
And so on, back through history.
Malthus the Malshapen, The Necromancer Grimm—

COMBE

I sought, through the study of dead languages, to become
worthy and adroit. Central to these lives of mine:
a concern for religion and its adherents.

DEMON

As in gummed labels?
You were, for a thousand years at least,
a series of Churchmen, all of them fat. Your soul
with two strands twines: gluttony and the clergy.
A succession of leering porcine equivalents,
given to flatulence and vague cosmologies.
Some few lives you spent as Eurasian dormancies:
Monks. The Carpathian Fat Boy. The Ah Ching Fat Boy.
Then a Chinese gentleman, Wo Hung Too Fat,
who carried a Frisson Pipsqueak for a lap dog.

COMBE

I recall. They found me in a field of night soil.

DEMON

Now *there's* a euphemism. Evolved like the horse
(a theory of dwarfism in reverse) with time you became
in body big enough to form the background
for your own foreground.

COMBE

I was once a dwarf?

Demon

Chubbytail Enshicktlesho, a man of tragic height.
Your lineage we can trace, back through the race
of Narwhal and Oxgore, to the last of the dinosaurs,
a fat one called Hadrosaur Incipitant. And beyond,
all the way back to the creatures of the Burgess Shale.
Always at their Cambrian grab-ass—Oh, how they played!
Always, of course, in pursuit of their aquatic beef roast.
Like animal tracks, yours is a past that pointed to a future.

Combe

This is like a dessert with too many ingredients,
a compote with more than the mind can retain on its stomach.
What's wrong with fat? If *bears* do better, fat,
why not folk?

Demon

I don't know, do you hibernate?

Combe

A supper may bust our belt, but by next morning
we see it cooked down into what we were last night—

Demon

We don't use the royal "We" here,
or were you counting your stomach as a second party?
Will there be two for dinner tonight? I understand
how the waist of a man in middle age thickens
with satisfaction, but this is ridiculous.

Combe

As bread is a vehicle for butter, so is butter
a vehicle for salt. As butter adds dignity
even to cheese on its cracker, so the coagulated
good of grease—

Demon

Hamburger patties? You ate them by the Holstein.

Combe

To eat the flesh of the crustacean and call it square—

Demon

Whole species you ate to extinction.

Combe

We need main *courses.* A nice onion pie.
It was a memorable flake pie withal—

Demon

You were a man powerless before his appetites.

Combe

I was a man powerless before his appetites.
I am so depressed I could eat a haruspicated corn-dog.
I feel so fat and told about.

Demon

It is not unusual
to go through these periods of identity agog.

Combe

It's like living inside a body balloon!
The body of man is oily and heavy. Bundled fat.
A seal in the surf for the Great White's play.

Demon

Now what do you suppose dat adipose is up to,
how all de time it want to sheathe de body in fat?

Combe

Where *is* that upstart pipsqueak of a poet?
He was ripe and ready for the hanging

when he tried to escape—on a flying machine!
He was last seen pedaling like hell
into the battering wind sets of a hurricane—
shuttlecocked from weather front to weather front.

DEMON

I haven't seen him but Hell, you know, is one big place.

COMBE

Intemperance was my sin. Intemperance
and colic. I thought a boatload of indigestion
was my penance. But you said that a soul
is a set of passions projected through a lot of time.
So what's the difference between appetites and passions?

DEMON

Good question. The appetites ensure survival.
Hunger and lust, they move men to do what they must,
by ones and by kind, to persevere. But appetites
are not informed by values, are not way stations for the soul.
Passion is about the giving of the self
to something other than the self. From passion
informed by values comes character. Passion
is about giving, appetite is taking.
Appetite is passion's homunculus.
Having the one, Fatso, does not give you the other.

SCENE 3. THE ITINERANT POKER

DEMON

Let the games continue! Let's play True or False.

SOUL 1

Let's not.

DEMON

Very well, how about riddles?
"Not belly not back not butt, I store my mammal fat
in my penis." What am I?

SOUL 1

A big dick with wings.

DEMON

OK, what is the *second* largest user group of bobby pins?
Give up? Jewish men, to hold their yarmulkes in place.
Did you hear there's been an explosion in the *déjà vu* factory?
"Anybody hurt," you ask? Three memories and a recognition.
All right, what about a hand of Locust?

SOUL 1

Your game is this:
To get me to speak from the throat of despair. You want me,
as a bicycle pours forth on its moment of imbalance,
to pour out the major eventetudes of my soul.
Then from this most abject summation of my life
you will use the considered opinions of the steam-driven world
to release the coiled springs of remorse. You want from me
the politically-corrected decisions of the guilt-stricken.

DEMON

No, no. We are always interested to hear from a man
at peace with himself. Besides, I hear the dark clutter
of someone who thinks he has something to say.

Soul 1

You see in me
An unattractiveness pronounced and particular.
But what is there to feel guilted about? What's good? What bad?
What right, wrong? In the operating theater of the soul,
you would dissect the substructure of the impulse.
In a cloak of knowing, by the candlelight of equivalence
you want me to renounce the proceeds of satisfaction.
You want to see a recitation of remorse.
My deepest belief is that it doesn't matter.

Demon

No, no. As the Hessian gunner says, we aim to please.

Soul 1

I find the both of you as brain dead as a cattle car.
You, a one-time hombre of upper-air superiority,
now try like a crow to complain the dog away from his food.
And this, this Glutton for punishment: Unlike him,
who *I* was I can recall quite vividly.
Perhaps that is part of *my* punishment.
I was Flavian Wyoming—

Combe

Why should your mangy bio be of interest to *us*?

Wyoming

I sang the body eclectic. The mammalian overpoise.
I sang of potency and act, essence and being.
Call it the blustery *etoo*, the exculpier *fonfado*.
The huge *nethingness* of *narcoltwist*. Not
to be underestimated, in force it's right up there
with the power of water to shatter granite when it freezes.
I was in life a frequently priapic man;
time and again I touched the fire hole called Proclivity.

COMBE

Spare us the details of your enravishment.
If the Maker gave you a cloven base
it's no concern of mine.

WYOMING

Eons ago
I was of a people who lived close to the loins,
Lake Dwellers at the glacier's mouth—

DEMON

The Ice Age breeding stock of Central Europe.
Assembled from Getes and Danes,
an Irish famine farmer or two, in fact
you were the leader of the Dilds,
a people of ingenious tools,
who comprised the Kingdom of Güsh.

WYOMING

I was a man of the homoveldt variety.
And I was unstoppable, ever the lover
of the furry female underfold. They called me Caveman:
If she'd make a tent of her body, I'd be the pole.
Even back to the dinosaurs I was
always in search of prime Devonian shatstock,
always ready to give it my bestial best.

DEMON

And after the Dilds, what life?

WYOMING

You know I was Paris.

DEMON

Helen! Oh *do me, do me, do me* Helen.

Wyoming

Helen. The smooth line of her cheekbone's palisades . . .

Demon

(The face that sank a thousand ships.)

Wyoming

. . . the great construct of her hair . . .

Demon

(Her hair,
as red as if she rose from a burning bed,
an erotic embellishment, a flag of piratic intent.)

Wyoming

I was the beaut-i-fully manlike of my kind,
she the beaut-i-fully womanlike of hers.

Demon

(The thunderstruck beef boy and the dark-carved gown.
Dressed to kill she walked in a salt of symbols
of her kind, her time, a litter of inducements.)

Wyoming

I laid her, on our wedding night, in a phalanx of pillows.

Demon

(There in the dark, Paris's peter, a loaf long,
no longer had the harbinger hang.)

Wyoming

Together for the first time, flesh to molded flesh . . .

Demon

(Spread wide, she waited to found a dynasty.)

Wyoming

. . . together we rose to the mammal melting point.

Demon

(The mammal *mmm*. He dispatched her with elegant shoves.
Bespoke. Bespoke. 'spoke. 'spoke.)

Wyoming

And she gave Paris all she was capable of.

Demon

(*Ohee, Yo-aa, Uh-huh, Oii Oii Oaa Oaa Oii Naa huh Oh Oi ah ah.*)

Wyoming

After, she schooled me in the muss and misuse of hair.
And I enfolded her, I was her slumbery penumbra.

Demon

(A jerk of the means brought them to their perfect
form, the crystal implant, the end of chance.)

Wyoming

A marriage of potential and potential, our confidences
numbered in the hundreds of pillowgrams.

Demon

(He talked, she talked, quietly exchanging other people's thoughts.)

Wyoming

Helen had been cultured like a pearl.

Demon

(Helen priced herself like a colony.)

Wyoming

On the dunes of Troy two versions of the future
of our kind came together for a third.

DEMON

(If there is a poetry of ovulation, she was writing an epic.)

WYOMING

I hate it when ladies die. I have this love for them.
I love their kind, great in its attributes.
Even as diadem for the wealthy man
they are more than ornament.
Even as panacea for the baker's boy,
more than fornicatrix.
As poseur for the butcher's, more than fox.
Women, whom we would gather to us and protect.
Women, whom we love for their *gentillesse*.

DEMON

(Helen, now of Troy. Helen, late of Troy.)

WYOMING

The two of us made the total sacrifice . . .

DEMON

. . . of everyone around you. Was it all downhill from there?

WYOMING

Giuseppe Herehecomes, a crazy Italian.
Petroleon Havockstick, a crazy Russian.

DEMON

(A gawky, infiltrated cosmockapole.)

WYOMING

Emile Peckerchance, a crazy Englishman—

DEMON

We have a typo. I show it as Peckerdance,
also known as The Itinerant Pecker.

Wyoming

No, that should read Itinerant Poker.
Then I was an apostle of Climaxology:
the study of apexes, summits, overages;
of apertures and their invasion by intrusion;
all with their attendant Hosannas and Alarums.
It was early science. I don't remember his name.
From there it was clear sledding to Lothario.

Demon

Lothario! What an exponential spread
of dirtiness you made of your life and times.

Wyoming

It is true. I was the life of my times.
I did large numbers of women.
I was ever ready for the fearsome frolic.

Combe

What was it like, to be famous for such a thing?

Wyoming

Like playing dodge ball with the devil.

Demon

On bedsprings, twice a second you made the cricket chirp.

Wyoming

Making love on fine furniture in drawing rooms:
We called this "Printing the Fortuitan."

Demon

You had a gift for crotchifying any conversation.

Wyoming

I loved the long-sought lace, the paroled acknowledgment.
I lived for the *doily dupta*, the *unh* and *ah*.

COMBE

What impresses me is how people will fuck tirelessly
for practice, in order to be ready to fuck for procreation.

WYOMING

Did you pick only one thing from the menu, Fatso?
My happiness required a steady supply of *Mooktar poontang.*
Not for me the married games of cat and spouse,
where kisses are expectations, not discoveries.
What does a man *do* with a wife anyway?

COMBE

As much as possible?

DEMON

Your wand wanted variety.

WYOMING

From the merest maid, chewing the bone of contention,
to the occasional philanderess, to the high lady
with whom it was never less than a pirouette with peril.
The latter was how I came to make this latest trip.

COMBE

Man is wont to treat as object the woman he desires.
Rather you want to tenderize, to center her soul
in the substance of what it is you want to do. After all,
for her her body is the baby carriage of her soul.

WYOMING

So my "sin" is that I treated woman
not as à person in her holistic entirety,
but only as recipient for the Yed flesh?
If there is an applauded place for pure love,
why is there not a place for lust unconfused by "love"?

Combe

To make love, to be in love.
Why does the word confuse such different things?
Is a man capable of both at once?
Is this not what marriage achieves? Body and body,
soul and soul: the perfect union an "and" and "and."

Wyoming

If love is the spiritual counterpart of lust,
what is the spiritual counterpart of gluttony?
It doesn't sound good for you, Rotundamento, does it?

Demon

Lust. It comes from a different organ than the heart . . .

Wyoming

. . . and is sooner vented. Lust has its place.

Demon

In the barnyard, per exemplum.

Wyoming

In the bed,
the back seats of cars, restaurant rest rooms,
on factory floors, in hospital corridors.

Demon

So a man
is separated from the world by the length of his dick?

Wyoming

A man is as *close* to the world as the length of his dick.
Woman lives at the center of our universe:
Women are to be watched and honored.
They know this, and this is fine with me.
I bring them my need, my springy male necessity.
They answer with the spongy needs of their kind.

Demon

Oh, the mutual consent of it all.

(To the tune of "Buffalo Gals.")
Two-ton Mary, won't you sit on me tonight,
sit on me tonight, sit on me tonight . . .

You are in your appetites quite predictable.
This is the ho-hum of addiction.

Wyoming

If much of the time
there was an electrical fire in my pants, so what?
I did what my glands impelled me to do. I have,
in my life, released jillions of intemperate sperm.

Combe

And that's just one life!

Demon

Yours is an unremarkable
descendre, an uninhibitable *deboo.*
What do all these men that you were suggest?

Wyoming

They can jack off six to a boat for all I care.

Demon

We had Onan through here a while ago.
Couldn't stop touching himself. Finally I asked,
"Can you learn to sit without playing with yourself?"
"I don't know why they call it playing with yourself,"
he said. "Working with yourself is more like it.
I've got a little current here; I can complete
the magic circuit all by myself. And by the way,
if masturbation were a hanging offense,
there wouldn't be anyone left to do the hanging."

"But can you be happy," I asked, "in a world of one-way mirrors?"
"Confronted with fact," he said, "the fantasy always seemed better.
But can you imagine going down in history for *this*?"

COMBE
To end in the dead end of a pulled pud. What *is*
the happy life? A few orgasms and a lot of laughs?

WYOMING
A lot of orgasms and a lot of laughs.

DEMON
You are men of quite incurable appetites.
Your appetites are your gods.

WYOMING
What's to cure? What to feel guilted about?
Live without appetites? To *live* is to hunger.
It's what lights a person, like lightning, from within.

Scene 4. A Momoyama Screen

Demon

Now there you have an elaborable theme.

Wyoming

Hunger. Without it life cannot endure.
If we don't eat we die. It we don't breed
the species dies. How then can it be a source of sin?

Combe

Appetite is Nature's way of signaling—

Demon

You're just a couple of appetites conversing.
Are the appetites a source of sin? A quick look
at the Seven Deadlies would suggest they are:
Lunacy, Prophesy, Lechery, Gluttony
(Are you taking notes, Fatso?), Profligacy—

Wyoming

You mean the Seven Lapses to Happiness.

Demon

At what point does hunger become preoccupation?
At what point does preoccupation become addiction?

Combe

When hunger ceases to be means and feeds itself.
When appetite becomes an end in itself,
when it becomes addicted to the addiction.

Wyoming

All eat to live, but the glutton lives to eat.

COMBE

I beg your pardon?

DEMON

Then are they "sins" of kind or of degree?

COMBE

Hungers can't be sins of kind. But yes,
in excess they would be sins of degree.

DEMON

As in *Nothing in Excess*?

WYOMING

So the Greeks would say.

COMBE

So do Christian and Classical converge.

DEMON

It's for moments like this I love these fireside chats.

WYOMING

But that's negative guidance. *Nothing in Excess*
tells us what *not* to do. Now what should we *do*?

DEMON

Can't you think of any second way to be?
Other souls stand here at the great divide,
where the predominance of science
or mysticism is anything but foregone.
Some few carve fine volumes out of space,
out of the unborn materials of song.
So (*Sings*) *How 'bout you*?

Wyoming

There's not much left to be disowned.
You know the lives I've lived, all narrow and enough:
How I made of each a flagrant testament.
But even I could glimpse the uneasy equilibrium
between yearning for the perfect life
and knowing the perfect life could never be.
It was with the *almost-not-at-all*
of pines in mist on that Hasegawa screen,
but I saw it all the same: What I glimpsed
was a world not free of appetites but not
in the service of them, either. A world
not just of the animalistic hand-me-down,
but one where spirit aspires and majesty inheres.
There was a kind of blue-sided triumph to it:
A world of proportion, and that a source of quiet joy.
To make much of a meaning from our life
is a matter of placing and presenting, of giving time
and a tempo to whatever we are given to.
You ask that I deal with the futures of my soul.
Renounce the hungers and their attendant pleasures?
I cannot and be human. But that does not preclude
the use of a life to make small islands of decency.

Demon

Acts of loving-kindness? I find those never to be boring.

Combe

I can't—for the life of me, I can't think
of any second way to be. To speak
of a moral life leaves the likes of me
one short step from sanctimonious.
More in my line is the alertness of predators,
the angularity of pests—and priests.
I'm here, you say, to select a future for my soul,
even perhaps a path to spiritual radiance.
But all I can see are the impediments.

I know, for example, that what we ask of clocks
we wouldn't ask each other: To be there,
to be precise, endlessly to be
on call and be correct. But turning that—
my little bit of just enough—to wisdom,
to the vision of a future—I'm not there yet.
I've chewed the hard beef of understanding.
It wasn't the best. It wasn't even good.
See how the sweat starts on my brow *as if.* My hands
reach out with the slight palsy of the terrified.

DEMON

The fraternization of the good
with what is merely trying to be good.
Oh ye of the quite articulated souls,
it is closing time in the Gardens of the West.
The sky begins to loosen and relent.
I see new clouds and a patripotestal lightning.
Soon there comes an animalistic rain.

Apotheosis Combe, I foresee for you
a chain of lives. You will sell
Weight Watchers franchises in Siberia,
and make a fortune selling a dietary chow
of soy flour and mutilated chicken parts.
When that life dies you will be reborn
a celebrity dietician. Your book,
The Abstemious Chow Hound, will expound
a new religion of eating:

> *To diet is to quarrel with one's body. Every bite*
> *a failure, every meal a Waterloo of the will.*
> *The trick is to jolt the calorie count*
> *from the declarative to the decrementalized.*
> *In my religion we stop after the appetizer.*

All rosary beads and adipose, you will be
a speaker at the National Obesity Conference.

But secretly, after the restaurant's close, you'll join
the *maitre d'* to feed intensively on leftovers.

COMBE

What is the end of that particular life?
Can I still be master of the Ring Ding supply?

DEMON

An early death and a probable life thereafter
as a cancerous sushi chef, serving pieces
of himself.

COMBE

If I'm blessed with a long life I'll do more.

DEMON

Hope requires a vision. Flavian Wyoming,
you are not without both. Master you will be
of The Shaker School for Wayward Girls
in Mount Lesbian, Ohio. There we will see
how you, in the exquisite tension of serving
human needs while needing to be served, will do.
But I foresee a scowling Alphonse, scowling Babette.

WYOMING

I say, if thy right hand offend thee, cut it off.
If thy penis offend thee—give it another chance!

(*Lightning flashes twice, all disappear.*)

Opcit en Afrique

Scene 1. Breaking News

Players
Natasha Ish, CNN Correspondent
Ibn Opcit, Poet-Fugitive
Idi Nakumbo, President, People's Republic of Usurpia

The scene is the capital of Usurpia, Africa's newest republic, on streets torn by civil war.

CNN Anchor *(Offstage.)*

And finally tonight, we bring you an exclusive.
CNN's own Natasha Ish, who never saw
a war she didn't like, has managed to become
the only correspondent to report
from the heart of Africa's newest civil war.
This one, a lulu, is in the West African
Republic of Usurpia. Natasha, can you hear us?
Is that gunfire?

Ish *(Sounds of machine gun and cannon.)*

Thank you, Brad, for your concern.
I hope you're also well, in that safe, warm studio.
I speak to you this morning from the city of Sores.
For a week, the battle for this once-beautiful capital
has raged. And the big news is, the government has fallen.
Rebel forces, under General Idi Nakumbo,
appear to have prevailed in the running battle of Sores.
In the fog of war, it's difficult to know much more.
There's shooting in the streets, burning cars,
corpses in the canals.
An eye-witness interview
could help us here. That should be no problem—
the streets are full of looters—Sir, sir!

IBN

The name is Opcit, Ibn Opcit.

ISH

You don't appear to be a local.
I was looking for a local.

IBN

I am a Poet-Fugitive escaped from Grace.
I carry the ruins of my country on my back.

ISH

I don't understand.

IBN

I took a wrong turn
at South America. The wind and water did the rest.

ISH

So you came here by boat? Are you a boat-person?

IBN

I flew here on a connivance of cordage and spry,
spar and stilt. Into lightning and thunder
I disappeared. With the urgency of Noah's dove
I strove for altitude, climbed the pummel of cumulous
to the jet streams. From icy sweeps of cirrus
I read the sea's face far below, like a planetary text.
At last this coast, in an early light
of indigos and lavenders, appeared.
Like a great begat I cleared the salt enfuddlement
of surf and slowly settled to earth.
The guards at the airport parapet kept watch.
Welcome, they said, lofting their steady beers.
Welcome to the State of Devastation.

Ish

So you are a poet, and you are *not* a citizen of Usurpia.

Ibn

I am as ownerless as an umbrella left in a café.

Ish

You picked an interesting war to visit.
What can you tell us? What have you seen?

Ibn

These weeks I saw a city under siege.
I heard the adumbrated Rattle Gun,
the thud of the big Ecclesiastes gun.
I observed, close up, the arts of evacuation,
the etiquette of street fighters. And I saw,
Miss . . . ?

Ish

Ish. Natasha Ish, CNN.

Ibn

And I saw, Miss Ish, great piles of dead.
The dead licking the dead.

Ish

Oh my God,
here comes General Nakumbo himself!
General, oh General!

Idi

You may call me President, President for Life.

Ish

I didn't know.

IDI

We had a vote today. My people insisted.
And you are?

ISH

Ish. Natasha Ish, African Correspondent,
CNN, and Chief Travel Editor, *Places Not to Go.*
I am here, Mr. President,
to report this war to a watching world.

IDI

Welcome, Miss Ish!
As the only person of your calling left alive,
you have a chance to give history its wings.
Welcome to the People's Republic of Usurpia!

ISH

Mr. President—if I may—why do people
call you Volcano Stripper?

IDI

They don't.
At least not to my face they don't.

IBN

(At most they would call him a change agent
with a weakness for magnificence.)

ISH

Isn't it true your "army" is really just a mob
of mercenaries?

IDI

Not for us, Miss Ish,
the physicalness of impromptu thieves.
What is wanted in an army: men reliably with guns.

IBN

(They are his Fortunate Marauders, paid to be aggressive.)

IDI

Do I know you?

ISH

He's with me, Mr. President.
His name is Ibn Opcit—he's a famous poet.

IDI

So . . . you two are an item? What a pity.
I was thinking, Miss Ish, that you might like
a *private* interview with a head of state—
who happens, also, to be one great caisson of a man.

ISH

Sorry, Mr. President, this is business.

IDI

Of course, Miss Ish, of course. In you, I see,
the female chromosome is lightly posited.

ISH

It's lightly posited throughout my line of work.

IDI

So true. These Runway Queens wear pants, weigh in—
they are confused. You are a newspaperwomanman.

ISH

Please, Mr. President, let the interviewer
organize the interview. Now what about
reports your troops have visited atrocities
on women and children?

Idi

Only those who fought back.

Ibn

(He buried them in such a way
that they will scream for centuries.)

Ish

I have reports of other atrocities.
Corpses hung from the loins of bridges.

Idi

I am shocked. Shocked.
A bridge should be known for what it spans,
not for that which depends from it.

Ish

Reports of bodies hung from the tops of flagpoles.

Idi

You're right, it's an odd way to salute the flag.

Ish

Even reports your troops fueled the municipal boilers
with the bodies of priests.

Idi

We couldn't find any bond salesmen.
Seriously, Miss Ish, here in Usurpia
there is a *slight* separation between church and state.

Ish

And what of your predecessor?

Idi

Enough, Miss Ish.
Enough. Your questions have a hostile rub,

and certain itchy dependencies require
my full attention. For now I think that you,
you and this friable boy of yours, should disappear.
Consider yourselves my honorary prisoners.
It may be, under the adroit hands of my questioners,
you will choose to confess. Then, in a weeping gape-cart
they will pull you through the streets to Restitution Square.
My hangman claims his nooses are like neckties,
with the slide of silk on silk. Guards!

SCENE 2. AIR FORCE 1½

PLAYERS
Nakumbo
Ish
Opcit
Spillman Sponneker, Vice President USA

An improvised banquet hall. Idi is preparing to host the Inaugural Lunch.

IDI

Not there, you idiots. I want the table *here.*
Let the band play *there.* Let the food be served
from over *here.*
(*Enter Ish and Ibn under guard.*)
Come in, come in.
You two are forgiven. How fortunate, Miss Ish,
that I am not one to dwell on grievances.
The days of countenance and sweating are over,
the need to be seen has become paramount.
(Gesturing to the smorgasbord.)
The pizza has found its place in the American diet.
The grapefruit has not.

ISH

May I quote you on that?

IDI

There is work to be done, and you each have a part.
Today, Miss Ish, is my Inaugural, and I
am in countdown fever for the festivities.
I want you to call in the cameras of CNN.
I want the world to witness this Inaugural!
To an angry Army drummer band beat the parade begins.
On a horse named Burning Hills I will lead
like Heraldry down Independence Rue,

thence by the Avenue of the Justified
to meet up with elements of our Armored Cav.
Behind will be a grand procession marked by
ululation, echolalia, glossolalia.
(Be sure to salute when the gondolas go by.)
Then tom-toms will amble with the beat of speak
and I will deliver my Inaugural Address.
It will, I assure you, be a moment knee-weakening
in excitement and enervation. As coda
to the entire affair, I am commissioning
an Inaugural Poem from our Poet Lariat.
(*Points to Opcit.*)

ISH

You mean "Poet Laureate"?

IDI

I mean Poet Lariat.
If Ibn Apeshit here does not come through
he'll wind up back at the end of my hangman's noose.
But you won't fail me. You wouldn't show me such ingratitude.

IBN

I am grateful for many things. I have not had my ears cut off.
Nor my nose. I have not had a hot poker inserted up my ass.

IDI

Early days, my poet friend, early days.

IBN

(Poetry is hostage to almost everything.)

IDI

But there is more. I've saved the best for last.
We are expecting a Most Distinguished Visitor
to grace our celebrations, none other than the President—
of the U.S. of A. himself! Not every day

does a fledgling African republic receive
such recognition. He is en route now.
I of course will host the welcome banquet.
You, Miss Ish, will record this meeting for history.
You'll chronicle my encounters with the great,
admire my suave and diplomatic feats,
the distillation of comradeship into acts of State.
And you, Apeshit, shall be . . . my Fellows the Butler.
The wine steward.

IBN

(They also wait who only stand to serve.)

(*Sounds of a heavy aircraft landing.*)

IDI

Zounds, that's him. Strike up the band!

(*The band strikes up "Hail to the Chief." Enter Spillman Sponneker, Vice President of the United States.*)

Welcome . . . Mr. President? May I say
you look somewhat younger than your photographs?

VEEP

And more handsome, I hope. I am Spillman Sponneker,
Vice President, and I bring hugs and kisses from our President.

IDI

But the plane . . .

VEEP

. . . is not Air Force One,
I came on Air Force One and One Half.

IDI

I am honored beyond belief, but your President . . .

VEEP

. . . regrettably is detained. Affairs of State, you know:
Founding the Federal Suppository,
passing the Fetid Air Act,
funding the dark side of the moon.

IDI

Of course,
we understand the dinkum of politics.
Fellows! Is the wine decanted?

IBN *(Filling his glass.)*

(No, but it's demented.)

ISH

Mr. Sponneker, is this "state visit"
not merely an attempt to divert
attention from your troubles back home,
your chaotic relations with a costive Congress?

VEEP

Congress? Those assertive bumble-boobs!
The United States Senate is peopled by one hundred
trained chinchillas. But you are . . . ?

ISH

Natasha Ish,
CNN, here to cover the Inauguration.

VEEP

General Nakumbo, I wonder if we might have
a word alone.

IDI (*MOVING HIS PARTY TO HEAD TABLE.*)

Of course, Mr. Vice President,
of course—but here are my guests arriving now.
Allow me to point out the dignitaries in attendance:

The entire House of Lawds, my consulting aristocrats;
the diplomatic corps, most especially Escondido
Amalfi, Special Envoy from Erluxia.
You see them in there fooding up, elbowing
and gamboling without a snicker of compromise?
My chef has done himself proud, notwithstanding
his rather extravagant claims for mint jelly.

ISH

Who are those rather colorful characters?

IDI

You mean next to Exculpate Redondo,
Secretary of Housing, Tourism and Fixings?
That will be General Per Diem,
until recently of the High Khyber Rifles.
We call him The Reusable Gendarme. On *his* left,
as pragmatic as a tusk and half as high,
Lagniappe O'No, Minister of Chicanery.
Rounding out my cabinet is Livorno
Bootlace, Director of the Bureau of Infighting.
And of course Vice President (But Not For Life) Mangle
Surcease. As colorful as a lance corporal, for $1000
he will allow himself to be embalmed on camera.

ISH

And those, in uniforms of different colors and indifferent sizes?

IDI

My Entebbe Enclave, from across the Indian Pond.
They play some of the very best pinochle in the world.
To maintain discipline you need a man efficient
as a buzz saw, and that is Napalm Smith,
late of the Unpopular People's Front.
There's *Jesus* Hectocktin, a humanista
who understands the role of concrete in structural collapse.
That burley stew of a man is Rufus the Depiliator:

the most Bessemer of wits, but usefully profane.
A specialist, in fact, in explosive semantics.
Beside him, a man prone to single-shot rifle fire,
a giant-killer name of Fetus Jack.
And Ruddy Kin Kow, a scrubby subaltern who fixes me
with the extreme proxmire of his regard. Weird but skilled,
he moves by his peripherals. (He bears watching.)
That other one, with the bright bark of tattoos on his forearms,
that's our medical man Secretions O'Boyle.
Oh, he's a prime Gilmore, one to put cyanide in the salsa.
Have some orange marmalade—it's the last gasp
of the British Empire, you know.

Ish

No thank you.
And over there, those men as large as phone booths?

Idi

You note their strength, their sheer physical abundance?
Those are my omnivorous Marauders.
The one who made of his face a mask, magical
with haunt marks, whose own body he defaced
with honor scars, that one's Midwa Midwala.
The one with the head like a shaped charge, that's
Papua Nitro de Palma. There's Strafe-run McGraff,
an old gunner of uneven dirt.
And East Jesus Hurleyman, who played
Left Davit for East Timor, and Greaser McFudd,
who played Left Lung for the Slobovians.
You should see them all at their mess, the teeth
of their mouths with iron-mongered fillings
fastened on their monster cuts. And Lord how they sing!

This lard load is owed to Ed.
But he blowed it when he waked up dead.

Ish

Tell us about yourself, Mr. President.

Idi

Early in life the military tuck, military brace.
I was of those who choose a life in uniform.
And yes, I go to University. There I took
(*slup, slurp*) intellectual replenishment.
What, no salt for the kidney pies?
I admire intellectuals. I don't consider myself one.
Although I oppose book-burnings, I would support the notion
of bonfires to burn all steel-slide guitars.
And I hate nesting bowls. I have just outlawed them.

Ish

Tell me about your campaign, how it began.

Idi

To a river boat at dusk (the *Buford T. Ousley,*
Captain Kurtz commanding), we came brandishing.
A dozen of us armed with Fire Dong musket
and Party Sword, we made it a raft o' seizure.
The Captain, a pedantic quagmire of a man,
hailed us crooked from insanity.
(*Oats and potatoes, Mr. Hall. Oats and potatoes.*
Or *Bits o' realm canvas—belts—buckles o' heap brass.*
Farthing pieces of fortunes. Dollar and a harf
o' yopper harm.) We old-fire the coal-head
(*Fall the main and shorten the form, Mr. Jones.*)
but much of a hold of steam it did not build.
Its one-lung engine, it need miss only a stroke to die.
On that stupid iron boat pushed by stupid
iron paddles down the Congo we came,
plying the ivory trade, the yellow and damask molars.
We called on the gunrunner with his rows of rifles.
(*These are all my children and they all do good.*)
We called on the rumrunner with his rows of juice.

(*These are all my children and they all do good.*)
We called on the slaver and his rows of women.
(*These are all my children and they all do good.*)
Down the Congo with its alluvial demands
we sailed, singing road kill songs, to Bayingville.

ISH

Bayingville? That's a Sahara away from the capital!

IDI

Out of uninhabited weather patterns,
the white spaces on your white-man's maps
we came, an anonymity of many feet.
In vans with visored windshields; jeeps
liberated from a passing safari; a truck
donated by Montifiori Cleaners; even
a fold-up portable bike—a bicycle writ small—
our legions came. Over a savannah
as wide open as an infiltration,
via unguarded crossings where they sell water by the kidney,
over a bridge of old planks polished by tires,
to the met macadam of Highway 95
we cooked along from Orionne to Traduce.

ISH

As you traveled, did your army grow?

IDI

Did it grow?
Have you seen how a forest fire moves of its own accord?
How trees, in a fellowship of fire, burst one
from another into flame? How it grew!
The fringe peoples of the North: the dim-witted
Bedouin, the Intifada who forge
forward in the holy hope of dynamite.
The forest peoples, who ape the native ape:
The Uxswich Cannibals, frogging through the trees by threes.

The Entrails Grabbers, recruited from the Bologna Tribe.
The Mea Culpa Mau Mau. The steely-eyed Mai-do-do,
so light on the ground and invasive they can run for miles.

Ish

Did you encounter no resistance from the populace?

Idi

Those who did not join us moved out like gazelle,
awaiting pursuit. You know how it is,
like speeders when the state police appear.
We're all guilty but we count on the law
of averages not to get picked out.

Radio

Delphinium Gunner Six Three Two, this is Easy Breezy.

Idi

That will be the insertion team. We are still dealing
with certain authoritarian districts, a few itchy
dependencies. This is Gunner, go ahead.

Radio

The entire football team is missing.

Idi

I stand corrected. *That's* about the Inaugural.
Where were we?

Ish

We were up to the fall of the capital.

Idi

What history will know as the Running Battle of Sores.
After a month of the time-honored art of plantation burning,
the occasional blown-up train, we came to a rain forest
out of which high-risers rose. On the skyline

there was a huge partisan glow; already
the sacked capitol of Sores had burned
down to a satisfactory angry red.
There was the microwave tower bright with signal,
there the criminal environs, the dog-eared tin
of shanty-town. (The cloistered rich in the cool,
shady villas of Petitionville were no more.) We waited.
The Very Pistol snorted in the early air.
Then street by street, house by house there were more
than a few bullet holes tendered in the wall.
Blett. Splott. Wanging a *ding*, the rounds
reported by ricochet. The air was filled
with hungry shrapnel. In the bullet-pocked haze,
the smell of burning camel fat—

Ish

Were casualties heavy?

Idi

You know, Miss Ish, it's hard to put a bullet
into someone so it stays. But our Carrion Patrols
were up to it, the hard work of one-on-one killing.
Combat, you know, gives death its lively edge.
At last all that was left was the Presidential Residential,
a cockamamie house of dressed stone, flemished gut.
Those inside, with napalm we gave 'em a *Mariposa Toast 'em Up.*
Then it was quiet, so quiet you would know
had someone inside moved a statuette.
We kissed the ground. The People's Republic of Usurpia
was born! Can you help me finish this Potage de Mon Frère?

Ish

There have been stories of widespread starvation.

Idi

Now that's not true! See for yourself the food lines.
Cowshit-and-kidney soup. A dog chow made

of disemboweled oryx and cavital cleansings.
Offal and oofle, all you can eat. Why times a day
we have these people undigesting themselves,
sometimes on gravel, sometimes on the floors.
Give a man too much, it disrupts his digestion train,
it leads to gelatinous misdemeanors on the carpet.
Besides, the end of eating is to stop
as soon as you can. Take it from the ancients:
Everything in Moderation means
Leaving Everything a Little Hungry.

ISH

And what of your predecessor?

IDI

Lucien Tabeau?

ISH

Was he not also President for Life?

IDI

He was. And I said, "I can work with that."
You need to know he was the kind of man
who doesn't take his hat off when he shits.
We found him in his toilet stall, in a sprawl of pants,
reading *Ten Reasons to Die Alone.*

ISH

I thought you two were friends.

IDI

We were, but that was before
our relationship unbuckled and fell apart.
He had no reckoning vision, whatsoever,
of what is new and could be next. I tried to be nice.
I gave him the Napoleon Options:

Get out of town.
Be taken over, with regrets.
Be taken over, without regrets.
I tried to reason. "I give you life," I said. "I shit you not."
I told him, here was a *fait*, and there an *accompli.*
And there was a *coup*, and here a *coup de grace.*
Then on his gray and settled head I placed a curse.
The hand behind the Handspittle Conspiracy,
the muck in the Muckden Livestock Conspiracy,
Lucien was a case of indecent until proven guilty.
But gendarme after gendarme, he protested innocence.
At the end he was 80 lbs of putrid defiance.

ISH

They say he was beaten.

IDI

He took a drubbing, oh, he took two.
But first they slathered him with Greek Wrestling Butter.
Then they beat him till he yielded a rose-colored bladderwater.
He danced like a high boy on arches double sprung.
Then a Biafran body rub, done with a garden hoe.
That put him in the double yurt position.

ISH

His face, they say, looked mis-assembled from different kits.

IDI

Then the manufacturer should be held accountable.

ISH

He looked half-drowned.

IDI

More like a dehydrated
pomegranate. A water-soluble fellow, he,
but it's hard to look dignified under water.

Ish

One account says he died by firing squad.
Another that he was *crucified.*

Idi

A crucifixion,
Miss Ish, is like a bad construction project.
We do have building standards around here, you know.
No, he had a heart attack but only half died.
He asked to be buried in his hiking boots "just in case."
Shot, he screamed, *The unused portion is returned!*
Then he died. What's that? Speak up, Miss Ish.
When one has a frog in one's throat, we say
one is in barnacle voice.

Ish

Where are the remains?

Idi

There are none, thanks to a crocodile named Fat Free.
But Tabeau had no complaints. He had a ten-rain lifetime,
and most of the tapir of his life had been used up.
You can start his bio anytime.

Ish

Let me just say
that parts of your story leave me incredulous.

Idi

That's just because you think I'm a no-good, good-for-nothing.
In what is bad of my life at least see what is good.
Mistakes were made. Close enough. Clear enough.
Fair enough. Without mistakes there would be no learning.
So the little dog shits. So what? Error, Miss Ish,
is the source of progress.

Ish

You beat your people
into shapes of terror and compliance.

Idi

The terror is already on the planet. We merely seek
to channel it so nothing of the suffering
should go to waste.

Ish

But you are so banal
about these persecutions!

Idi

Persecute, prosecute,
execute—for me they're all samo samo words.
As to the banal: Where there are no clowns, Miss Ish,
there is little chance of honesty.
This Cartesian flop-hat, do you think it's over the top?
And now, if you'll excuse me, you never want to be far
from a speech you're about to give. And I've had enough (*belches*).
It was that Canadian bean soup did me wrong.

Towards a Just Republic

When a man builds a stone wall, he will be gone
long before it is known how well it will last.
So, if he builds it well, he is doing the work
for its own sake and making his bond with the future.
If not, we will bring him back and entomb him in it.

My fellow citizens of Usurpia,
ladies and gentlemen of the Work Force,
I'm not here to sell you a bucket of rainbow.
Looking back on this country you are inclined to ask,
What happened? Where the Hell did *we* come from?
But second-guessing the Revolution will get us nowhere.
Think of how it was before. Descended from slaves,
slavelike, our people living on little curbwhile atolls,
fixing lorries with ball peen hammers. Even today
they make scant livings out of beer and recycled peanut hulls.

"Give a hungry man a fish," another President
has said, "and he will be hungry again.
But teach him how to fish and he will feed himself forever."
I say, "Teach a man to tie his own bow tie,
and he will be a waiter. But teach him to sing,
and he will be a singing waiter."

Ours is a people rich with chocolate brown distinction,
but ever the racial epithets get more subtle, more refined.
I see the Arab watermen, in love with brass
for its own farthing sake. I see the Lebanese
jewelers with neither counterpoint nor name.
They are as French as the water supply. (That interruption
today, by the way, was a Hindoo blockage.) Indians,
they don't have answers but they have carpets. I see
the whole merchant class with its Settled-in-for-Life look.
Disenfranchising them—all those of indeterminate
Eurasian Hispanic look—I do not mind.

They are different from us. Not of the same coagulants.
As a people we are too multi-plural, and they are ass tripe.

When does a tribe become a people become a nation?
When it sees that "Nation" is the end of "Indignation"!
Life, liberty, and the ability to conceive
a condition of happiness, if not to pursue it.
The new order is *there* for the imagining.
The future belongs to those who show up!

Does Brother Python mistake the pig, passing through,
for an embolism? Does Brother Croc mistake
the hamstrings of our citizens for dental floss?
Is grass important to a golf course? Did Al Capone
wear a wedding dress? Of course! Of course not!

Today I take a stand on the high-risers
of Humility. I seek a renewal of innocence.
I don't know where we're going, but I know we can't stay here.
This much seems clear: whatever was, was *is*.
And what will be, different from what was, is *is*.

Out of the shallows of misgovernance
to work for the Constitution as a next-in-line,
to make of all this a surviving enterprise:
No dream that burns so bright could burn for long,
our critics say. They call it parchment blarney.
But slowly, like a clay cup in a kiln,
we find the ability of heat to harden and enhance.
Start the tom-toms with the beat of speak.
From could to can. From must to will!
With bias toward none and prejudice for all,
I declare a national holiday: The Nevermind Day!
This is a vacation for absolutely everybody!
And this is only Saturday. Think of Sunday!
Think of Monday! *To* this, *for* this
I make the prayer of a hundred years.
The Get Ready. The Get Set. The Go.

Scene 3. Table Talk

Still the Inaugural Lunch, Nakumbo is back with his guests.

Veep

Mr. President, I wonder if *now* we might have that talk?

Idi

Miss Ish! Fellows! Please withdraw yourselves.
(*Winks at Ish.*) Affairs of State, you know.

(*Ibn and Ish retire behind a screen, where they continue to listen.*)

Veep

General Nakumbo, allow me to come to the point.
I bear the burden of my President's concerns . . .

Idi

But tell me, how *is* your President? We haven't met
but I've read his biography, *Tales of the Optical Child.*

Veep

Bill Clapper? The man is not to be believed.
Most men in his position would be coasting
to their place in history by now. He should be working
on his memoirs (*Scrapes and Near Misses*).
But Bill Clapper wants the more, the most from life.
"Less is more," he likes to say, "but more is mucho."
Long after hours I've seen him in his Ovary Office,
hands clasped behind, brooding on his greatness.
He is haunted by the fear his Presidency
will be remembered as the Clapper Dormancy.
He compares himself to other presidents:
"Sometimes they do well, sometimes they do not
cop even enough magnificence to make a mark."
He complains the times have not afforded him

occasion to show his greatness. "Everybody's busy,"
he frets, "the rich becoming famous, the famous rich.
This could be as bad as the British Empire
with its long *oods* of stability: While the sun
can't figure where to set, they see how green
the lawn can get, how small the dollhouses can make."
I ask him, "Is it not enough to be seen to serve
the people from bended knee? Through a semblance of caring,
through great shows of attention, to go down
in history as a friend of the forlorn?"

IDI

Forgive my candor, but your man appears to be
as self-infatuated as a knot.

VEEP

Oh, you don't find an ego like that every day.
It's part of our cultural heritage. If this were Japan
it would be a Living National Treasure.
But you know politicians. They apportion
their rations of selfishness into like-appearing
rations of selflessness.

IDI

I know about
the politicians in your country: The only people
who want those jobs are those who should not be allowed
to have them. Here in Africa it's more of a calling.

VEEP

We are all of us angling for destiny,
but sometimes the opportunity *is* the motive.
For a time he played the forgotten Beauregard,
sat around in positions of needful neglect
counting the days of his incumbency.
One night he lugged his heavy body to bed.
An hour later he came running down.

"I had a dream!" the President proclaimed.
"A crowd in demonstration, shouting and waving signs,
all of which were blank!" He broke into a sweat.
"How do we use this office to pull things, aright or awry?
It must be simple, it must be hard to disagree with.
It must show cleverness and character."
His testicles, those small oracles
that never fail him, were talking now.
"It's time," he smiled, "to play the twinkle game."

He dove into books, he read up a storm in search of ideas:

The History of the Twenty-One Gun Salute.
The Value of Impulsive Punishment.
Bombings Aimed at Negligible Times.
The Politician as Lower Life Form: The Art of Staying Alive.

There was a sprouting of nomenclature.
The machinery of hokum moved into high gear.
In and out he worked the clutches of power
in a power appliqué. He checked with the boys at State
(the *Yes . . . Well . . . Maybe . . . But* bunch). To every hindrance
he declared, "I don't give a global, globular dammit."
(He can be as organizing as a belt when it finds its buckle.)
He convened his Cabinet. He belabored
his Secretary of State Ercott Nonothingnot,
for a list of Legacy Initiatives:
Item: To protect the planet from Ainu attack.
His Secretary of Labor Denise Maltfalcon
for a list of Policy Initiatives:
Item: To decry the slow extinction of calligraphy.
His Secretary of Culture Arbuthnot Yo Yuppynot:
Item: To create a national war poetry.
"It's an expensive matter to generate war poetry," he mused.
"Sending off a generation of 20-year-olds . . .
and what have you got then? A return on investment
that's slow and uncertain—a few books 20 years later.

No, it's a costly, risky enterprise
to build a national art, war by war. Keep going."
He consulted the Center for Global Annoyance, the surmise guys
with their Latinate gobbledygook.

IDI

Academics.
They are the fart-flowers of civilization.

VEEP

Yes, but it was they who gave him his idea.
It was one of those moments when the proxies come together
with a grin. What they found was, he has done nothing in Africa.
"Africa," he said. "Find me a civil war.
There must be at least ten. Find me a good one."
He checked his five-day venereal planner. He booked
a prime-time speech. He put on his bejeezus demeanor.
"My fellow Americans, under my policy
of military might for a rainy day . . ."

IDI

And what does that make *us*? A far square inch
of ownership on the Oval Office globe?
Why couldn't he just stay home and teach the Arapaho
how to shoot straight?

VEEP

He didn't think of that.
But that, right there, that would alienate
the entire Ludovickian establishment.
The essential skill of a gunfighter, as you know,
is not the speed of his draw but his ability
to pick the right fight.

IDI

You Americans,
always needing to do the affrighted good!

VEEP

A politician's rhetoric is like a swizzle
stick. Its purpose is to stir things up.
After his address he made a salt of telephone calls.
Then he summoned me and said, "Get dressed up
in the coat and tie of settlement, take your plane
and personally deliver this message to Usurpia:
The President sends greetings to his black children.
To General Nakumbo he says, You can wait
for the thunderstorm to tell you what it thinks,
or you can get out of the rain."

IDI

He couldn't put that in writing?

VEEP

Anger in writing seldom preserves well.

IDI

As in your Declaration of Independence?

VEEP

What we need is to show the President as World Statesman.
We need to unveil, through American intervention,
an era of unrivalled calm in Africa.
What we would like, *President* Nakumbo,
is to offer you a territory swap.

IDI

You're here to adjudicate the line-stops of our borders?

VEEP

No, no. We thought you might like to breathe
the fresh air of a foreign land.
You would step down as president of Usurpia
in favor of a successor we would name. In return
we would offer you a sovereign territory

of equal value. We were thinking of a quiet place
somewhere in the lesser corners of the earth.
Cuba, perhaps. We were thinking of Guantanamo.

IDI

The whole of Guantanamo? Guantanamo entire!

VEEP

We could throw in something else.
The Patrice Lumumba National Park?

IDI

Do I sense a certain Heraldic overreach?
Won't the current owners have something to say?

VEEP

We can persuade them to let go of their vigorous entitlements.

IDI

You offer me a hopeless half-acre on Hell's estate . . .

VEEP

I'm here to help if you will have my help.
How about islands? We have some in our portfolio.

IDI

I was thinking of something closer to home—your home.

VEEP

You don't mean the earthly paradise
of North America itself!

IDI

How about Maine, that choice piece of Canada?

VEEP

Maine is our long fist of protest into the vitals
of Canada. We could never offer that.

IDI

Then could we consider the dry basins of the Southwest?

VEEP *(Ironically.)*
Why not throw in Nebraska.

IDI

Let it be Nebraska.

VEEP

There is not a China-person's chance in Hell of that.

IDI

It seems very unlike, to send me to the other side
of China with a pile of furniture.

VEEP

Your furniture?
Why, it would transport as easily as your two balls.

IDI

So. With the conviviality of a land grab
you would convert me to a stateless epicure.
Whom should I thank? To whom should I give my *Nothing Doing*?

VEEP

Shall I take that as your final word?
You refuse to part company with your country?

IDI

You may take that as my rum response:
Nothing, nada, rien—and *nix*.

VEEP

Now, there's no need to get beefed up and bothered.
Drivers work things out at 4-way stops,
And so can we. We need to work this out.

IDI (*Holding out his glass.*)
Fellows, get out here! Strong drink, and keep it coming.

ISH (*Ibn and Ish still behind the screen.*)
He's calling you. What are you going to do?

IBN

I'm going to answer back.
I'm going to give him some of what he gave us.

ISH

That you mustn't do. If you want to stay alive,
you will smile and bow, and you will serve the wine.

IBN

We stand here like a wooden city on a windy day,
holding our breath—for fear of fire. Will *that* keep us alive?

ISH

If you confront him, you don't know what he'll do.

IBN

Oh, I think I know.

ISH

He will act with venom and dispatch.

IBN

Probably, they'll make macramé out of my guts.

ISH

Then why do it?

IBN

There is a part of me that will not be owned.

Ish

You can obey him if that's what it takes to stay alive.
You can show him weakness and beg for mercy.

Ibn

From *him*? When Sponneker leaves,
we'll be buried in a field of night soil.

Ish

If you provoke him, you make that a certainty.

Ibn

The fine close work of trying to stay alive.

Ish

Why do you do this?

Ibn

So that which he craves will not be his to have.

Scene 4. 4-Way Stops

The lunch continues.

Idi

Fellows, where are you! Bring food. Bring wine!

(Ibn enters bearing an enormous tray. Ish remains behind the screen.)

Ibn

Milords and ladies, it is a thing surpassing suave,
surpassing sage, that you allow me to serve you today.
For our pleasured guests we start with a jasmine
of cold wine and cucumber finkle.
For entree we have Filet de Castro and a piece
of Companion Fish, followed by a dish of Hopscotch Pudding.
The wine is for nothing.

Veep

No thank you, I ate on the plane.

Ibn

A light repast, perhaps? Gravlax and Kumamoto?

Veep

We had a Mexican dinner on the plane;
the fiesta in my stomach kept on going, all night long.

Ibn

A Mexican meal still barnstorming through your body?
Is your stomach blundering toward its anal finale?
Not to worry, we are placing the contents of your toilet
in the holding tank for Biohazardous Waste.

Veep

What are you, a medical experiment?
Has there been a hang fire in your gene pool?

Idi

We like our employees a little impaired, a little
crippled. Fellows, just the wine for now.

Veep

President Nakumbo, our relationship
with your predecessor, Lucien Tabeau,
was based on avarice, cunning, and mutual mistrust.
I trust we'll have the same success with you.
My President has authorized me to make
a second offer, should you decline our first.
What we would like is to enlist you in the FDPP.

Idi

The what?

Veep

You've heard of our Federal *Witness* Protection Program?
Well, this is our Federal *Despot* Protection Program,
also known as the Husha Buydown. There comes a time
in the life of every Tin Pot Tyrant to sort out
his cross-hatchings of ownership and dictatorship.
If the role of government is to make as many as possible
as happy as possible, why not start with Number One?

Ibn (*Audible aside.*)
(The tyrant, he agrees and he starts with himself.)

Idi

Well I'll be a clapped hat on a monkey's head.
This has what they call in the business "possibilities."

Veep

All those other Presidents for Life,
they signed up the way peas accumulate in the pod.
Where do you think all those Presidents
of South Vietnam went to? Do you really think

Idi Amin lives in Saudi Arabia?
Robert Mugabe . . .

IDI

. . . of Zimbabwe?
Do you know that man is a patriot?
He loves his country as himself. He even wants
to rename it Robert Mugabe Enterprises.

IBN

(Quisling kings, they play the ancient game
called Rot & Throw.)

IDI

In local pubs they say
it is a source of song to push the cash across the bar.
What do you have in mind?

VEEP

In the FDPP are hecatombs of comfort.
We'll make it full of cashews and good things for you.

IDI

How *did* the world come to be so chock full of cashew nuts?
Fellows! A day without wine . . .

IBN (*Refills Idi.*)

(. . . is like a bird that can't defecate.)

IDI (*Sniffs and savors the wine.*)
Black cherry. Pear. Asparagus. Notes of barnyard.
(He farts wetly.)

IBN (*Sniffing*)
Black cherry. Pear. Asparagus. Notes of barnyard.
(Offers the wine.)
Mr. Vice President?

VEEP

Perhaps a cup of coffee.

IBN

We like to serve the coffee at room temperature.
It keeps the guests from hurting themselves. How about
some Baked Alaska? Here we call it Frozen Africa.

VEEP

You're more insane than Earl Mototny.

IDI

I've always been willing to follow the logic of the Assembly.
Which border did you have in mind?
I could not consider going North.

VEEP

Something better. In the Islands of Assent
stands the tropical paradise of Bent Peter.
There, to live in self-regulated governance,
our despots come. Guaranteed freedom from extradition,
you will play Parcheesi with tyrants of similar views.
You are allowed to bring all your belongings,
both personal and public. Numbered accounts,
wife or wives . . .

IDI

Could this include Copernica Catnip?

VEEP

Women with breasts like grain sacks, if you like.
We could also find room for your Cabinet—

IDI

I think it's simpler if I own everything.

Veep

Oh, I almost forgot: to all of this we add
an annual emolument equal to
several times your country's GNP.

Idi

Payable in gold?

Veep

In quantum ingots of the stuff.
For the rest of your life you'll walk around
expensive stores and feel superior.

Ibn

(Consider it movie money for a head of state.)

Idi

But Usurpia is not a week old.
What will historians say of Idi Nakumbo?

Ibn

(Oh, they'll be pretty specific in their gusto.)

Veep

Of course your abdication will occasion comment.
But we've anticipated that as well in A.I.M.,
our After-Image Management program.
As a comb organizes hair, we organize
public opinion. Sunday talk shows, editorials,
the works.

Ibn

(They'll make you a place in history
beside the likes of Mussolini in the scrapbooks.)

Idi (*Feeling the wine.*)
Fellows! A little of the Barley-Fly if you may.
(And hold the comments.)

Veep

That's a jeroboam of magnijohn.
What are you, a one-man cocktail hour?

Idi

So much good fortune. I must be being set up.
You offer me the key ring to the keys
of my kingdom, forgetting I need only the keys.
No. My answer must be No.

Veep

Some people mistake kindness for weakness. You have missed
the distinction between my helping you and telling you.

Ibn

(First the carrot, now the stick. First
the gravy train, now the powder train.)

Idi

Well, you know, I don't quit when I should. My answer's No.

Veep

Then we'll make of this city of Sores a beachhead for Hell.
We'll leave your country like a battlefield
scarred for life, until geology itself
will have to make amends.

Idi

It's always a special time when countries go to war.

Ibn

(And when both sides believe that God is on their side,
that makes for a good war.)

Veep

A Trident missile
Is something most people want to keep asleep.
What will you say when the last warhead has detonated?

Idi

We came from the mountains, jaggy with outcome,
and there we can go back.

Veep

So what's it going to be,
the welfare state or the warfare state?

Ibn

(If it's going to storm
and bunghole, let it be the Mother of All Wars.)

Idi *(Shouting at Ibn.)*
Will you shut up, you miserable cockroach!
I'll give you a drubbing, oh, I'll give you two.
You'll be the poet with the caved-in head.

Veep

Poet? I thought he was your wine steward.

Ish (*Emerging from behind screen.*)
How you two go on—it's like walking in
on organized crime. You're both insufferable:
The Camel Whipper and the Grand Guffaw.

Veep (*In wonder.*)
Well I'll be a kneeling bus.
That was very polarized, very full
of journalistic feeling.

Idi

If it isn't "Breaking News."
Still swinging at the piñata of public opinion?
You and your poet pal will soon be back in jail.

Veep

I have no dog in this fight.

IDI

Spillman, you can board that plane right now
if you've a mind to. Report to your Chief
the failure of diplomacy. Tell him you got here late—
the war you came to end I just had won—
so you came home. Then tell him every government
on earth will be here in a week to offer
recognition to Usurpia. And, Spillman,
do you know the reason for their amity?

VEEP

Because they want the ocean of oil beneath our feet?

IDI

And when your Chief asks how it came to be
that you came home without the oil when,
Christ Almighty, you had it in your *hand*,
what will you say?

VEEP

Our national honor is intact?

IDI

Spillman, have a seat and hear the deal that I *will* do.
You will become the valued ally of my government.
As a gesture of goodwill, you will give me
all those armaments you were threatening to use,
and I, in return, will give you first crack at the oil
so coveted by your allies. Your President
can enter history knowing he alone ensured
Usurpian crude would heat America.

ISH

Less, of course, a concession to cover your administrative costs.

VEEP

I find the logic insurmountable,
but the cost of all those planes and missiles—

IDI

We are dealing here in magnitudes
that for your country are a rounding error
of a rounding error. And to further
celebrate the makepeace of our nations,
I also will accept the trivial
lagniappe you offered earlier.

VEEP

You mean
the annual emolument, for several times
your GNP? That's outrageous.

IDI

Very well, as yet another gesture of goodwill,
I will release to you my hostage.

VEEP

Hostage?

IDI

Why yes: Miss CNN,
Natasha Ish.

VEEP

You offer me a single hostage?
That won't even make the evening news.

ISH

But I *am* the evening news!

IBN

Just a moment,
your Aggrieved Eminence. My name's not Fellows.
It's Ibn Opcit, and I am Poet Lariat.
I would be prepared to throw myself
into the hostage package as a bonus.

VEEP

Ipsit. Obbin Bobbin. Grogin Gripsit?
How is he pronounced again?

IDI

Ibn Opcit. Rhymes with village idiot.

ISH

He's with me—

IBN

and I'm a famous poet.

VEEP

A hostage release would be a coup, all right,
but the cost—

IDI

My deepest belief
is that it doesn't matter. I do, however, have to ask
what kind of car is in the FDPP package.

VEEP (*Consulting notes.*)
A Porsche Turbo. 512 horsepower,
332 foot pounds of torque and a great deal of tongue.
Alright, we'll give you the weapons and take the oil,
and give you the money and take Miss Ish.
But not the poet. We already have a Poet Laureate,
and poets are nothing but trouble to the State.

IDI

I compare the poet to the crocodile:
He shits in his own medium. But no problem.
We can always find a rope, and another
strangled poet more or less . . .

ISH

Just a minute, Mr. Sponneker.
I've heard everything—enough to guarantee
my Pulitzer—but I will not stand by to watch
while you two murder yet another innocent.
Or perhaps you'd like to hear the headline on my next dispatch:

Can Ocean of Oil Wash Blood Off America's Hands?

VEEP

I suppose we *could* find room for him on Air Force
One and One Half. We could let him out somewhere enroute—
how about it, Gripsit, can the wings of a poet
keep you aloft at 30,000 feet?
Or better yet, we could drop them both off
in the Soviet Union. That was my next stop anyway,
and *they* know what to do with poets.

IDI (*Shaking hands with Veep.*)
As to the offer of cookies in your package,
let me counter with Ben & Jerry's, a lifetime supply
of Raspberry Bosporus.

Scene 5. The Citizen at the End of the World

Ish and Ibn, back in their prison cell, await their fate. It is deep night, and Natasha lies on the only bed. Ibn stands at the single window looking out.

Ibn (*Mimics.*)
Well I'll be a kneeling bus. In Spillman we see
politics play the greasy handmaid to statesmanship.

Ish
I knew him in New Jersey, when he was lucky
to have a job as clerk in Ladies Underwear.

Ibn
Politics, that most cynical of all bespeakals.

Ish
Do you have a problem with all governments or just this one?

Ibn (*Mimics.*)
Government, they say, exists to make
as many as possible as happy as possible.
The demagogue agrees, and he starts with himself.
With here an *aplomb*, and there a *délicatesse*
he uses the frenzy of the jawbone
to make artful constructs of subversion.

Ish
Sponneker rode into office the usual way:
Mouthing platitudes, standing for things
three at a time, promoting virtues
as hard to find as last month's newspaper.
Promising to be all things to all people.
A branch for every bird that got a song to sing!

IBN

Demagogues are the insects of politics.
They live by sticky extrusions of body thread,
they coexist in crafty integuments.
Like water beetles they stay afloat
on surface tension; they taxi on iridescence.

ISH

Demagogues are like their campaign posters:
colorful, two-dimensional. What about dictators?
They don't have to please the voters.

IBN

Unacquainted with the stallions of compromise
the dictator gives the chosen shut-up; *his* constituencies
he aligns through the management of chaos.
His people he marches to the awarded tempo,
attended cadence until it is the death of custom,
the end of wonder. Out of his subjects the tyrant teases—
with chain fall and sledge—compliance and respect,
loyalty expressioned in the taken oath.

ISH

Does that mean we were better off with kings?

IBN

Kings of old, they taught our task was to behave
in whatever world we were given to.
Modern monarchs, mouthing the small bells of justice,
figure their ways, their wends, their intricate sends.
Beyond resolve, beyond relief, beyond belief
they confuse the rains, the reins, the reigns.
What all of them seek is to abrupt authority.
Bigger than a Constantinople Steeplechase,
they make their drastically-shaped enterprises.
They play the ancient game called Rot & Throw.

ISH

Is no man good enough to be a leader?

IBN

If a leader does not lead by example,
why should he lead by authority?
When Ibn sees a mounted general
in bronze, he asks, "What horse does that honor?"
There is a part of Opcit that resists
long marches straight ahead; that resists
the history of man as Learning Our Place.

ISH

It occurs to me we are both in the business of language.

IBN

Language: it's a great enabler to dishonesty.

ISH

Me, I fly from war to war, I interview
demagogues and potentates, warlords
like this one, hunkered over their defiant takings.
Language for me is asking *Why*, then writing *No*.
Is poetry dishonesty?

IBN

Poetry
can be its own worst enemy, much of it
rhythmic bromides, mere hymns of indifference.

ISH

How do you tell a real poem?

IBN

Writing a poem
is a fiercely independent act. The language
in a real poem will sound a new and savage

Flamenco—it will have the sound of sound
escaping from sense.

ISH

And what is a love poem?

IBN

A perfect immersion in the songness of the flesh.
It happens in that rare moment of sufficiency
when two together is entire and enough.

ISH

What are you watching that's so interesting?

IBN

The lean-down of the firmament. This African sky
has found its grasp of cloud and star. Clouds and stars
and a giant moon.

ISH

That sounds like a poem.

IBN

In the cursive shadow of eclipse
moon put on a paper face,
moon put on a paper gown.
And when the new moon come to town
it make a pregnant belly of the sea,
it gravitize a tide which gleefully
propound in its direction . . .

ISH

Ibn, do you have a girl?

IBN

That kind of companionship has not been mine.
Often I've known the need but never the opportunity.

(*Looking out the window.*)
It's dark out there, we're still in the midriff of the night.
The long, strong failing into day has not begun.
And it's cold. Very cold.

ISH

Then come here into bed.
Just to stay warm, you understand.

(*Distant sounds of heavy aircraft engines revving up.*)

The Last Cosmonaut

A Christmas Tale

Prologue

When Cosmonaut Sergei Krikalev finally gets back down to Earth next month—after spending seven months longer than he'd planned in space—he may well want to crawl back into his spacecraft.

He took off May 18 from the Soviet Union's sprawling Baikonur Cosmodrome in Kazakhstan. Twelve days before he was scheduled to return came the coup that set in motion the disintegration of the Soviet Union.

The space program got caught in the ensuing political turmoil. Once-lavish funds were withheld. Mr. Krikalev, whose flight was the subject of a page-one Wall Street Journal article, was pressured to stay up longer to save money on transport cost.

The country he blasted off from doesn't exist anymore. His hometown, Leningrad, has a new name. Space engineers are threatening to strike. Even the agency that sent him into space has been broken up.

The Wall Street Journal
10 February 1992

Day 1. Poets Shot from Guns

Players
Control 1, Mission Control
Control 2, Commandant, Baikonur Cosmodrome
Ibn Opcit, Cosmonaut

The last days of the Soviet Union. On a darkened stage, sounds of a rocket launch; a screen shows a Soviet rocket lifting off. Stage left, under a spot, is the control room of the Baikonur Cosmodrome. Stage right, under a spot, is Opcit in orbit. The dialogue is by radio transmission, with occasional static.

Control 1

Good morning, Comrade, and hail to the Soviet Supreme!

Cosmonaut

The name's not Comrade. It's Ibn Opcit. What I want to know,
when does the movie end and this plane arrive in Denver?

Control 1

Look out the window. That is no celluloid unroll.
That ball below you is earth. Turbulent, actual!
You are the guest to whom our Space Program is host!

Cosmonaut

Who is this? Is my face awake?
I want to speak to the object in charge.

Control 2

Yes. This is Gnurlybrow "Yuri" Tartaryavich,
Commandant of the Baikonur Cosmodrome.

Cosmonaut

What I remember: out of the snow a large man
clothed in canvas came. Like a closet promising
to impart secrets he drew near. He asked the time.

Sneezing, he atomized my reply. In his excuse
profuse, nothing would do but that he take me
to dry off at his favorite pub, *The Selective Pâté*.
Himself he introduced as simply "Commissar,
a servant's servant of the Soviet Supreme."
Gray suit, gray socks, he was dressed in utter gray.
Only his necktie had a multiple personality.
It was like last year's offense to humanity.
Like a bolt of light from another universe.
"Nice tie," I said. "Wakes up the suit."
He quaffed his quart of brew. "Alcohol," he said.
"Between some folk it makes for instant friendship."
Himself he described as a businessman of the sensibility,
a man of constant fiber and undone substance.
He recalled how, overweight and underfunded,
he sold Weight Watchers in Siberia.

CONTROL 1

I know this commissar. One of the clothespins
of our society. He can't come to the phone right now.
He's at home recovering from a mild case of hubris.

COSMONAUT

"So how do you make your living?" he casually inquired.
"By years of scratching in the dark," I said.
"What are you," he said, "an opal miner or a poet?"
"Both are extractive industries," I said,
"both relatively timeless enterprises.
But I'm in the business of verisimilitude.
In the grip of reality perceived, I write."
He smiled with a smile that did not include his eyes.
"This is splendid," he said. "This is fine."
Then he chortled and he buttoned up.
He pulled out his wallet like a fatted calf.
Nothing would do but that we have *another* drink
at *another* favorite pub, *The Impacted Centipede*.
A period of drunkenness must have ensued,

for Ibn lay down stress-free on the sidewalk.
The Commissar, he said he had a rocket "like a Porsche,
a sports car *molto dandy* called the Widow Machine.
Perhaps we can find room on our manifest.
This will be your quick way home."
The last words Ibn can remember hearing:
"Please step *all* the way into the People Compactor."

CONTROL 2
I suggest we get discovery out of the way.
To beer and vodka, Comrade, you succumbed.
You were impressed. The right ascension calculations
done, like a cameo in-load they packed you in.
Perhaps you heard the *bring* of the screw's threads
as they seated to the sides of the nut's flux.
They removed the metal treads. Then there was only
the vertical primness of the rocket on its pad,
15 or 20 times the height of a skyhook.

CONTROL 1
And you at its tip, like a shot waiting for the sling.
At the sulfureous, ramshackle flaring—like a match—
we declared "Ignition." Borne in a blare of fire
the rocket, heavy with matriculated light,
gained headway slowly if at all. But unlike
the last three it burned merrily and well.
Punched upward on the flame's blue thumb,
your face the very picture of stress, in the grip
of G's your weight became a hundredweight.
Down in your seat you shrank to the size of a space monkey.

CONTROL 2
Boosters slowly settled back and sank,
the rocket by stages emerged from itself.
In the tumble and grow of its fit with earth,
the satellite achieved the proper attitude.

Control 1

With inkling accuracy the poet Opcit
was posted to orbit. Welcome to Government Service.

Cosmonaut

Why me? Why a broken-down poet from the Caribée?

Control 2

Here at the Baikonur Cosmodrome
we feed at the neglected pump
of an indifferent public subsidy.
Who knows how to build these rockets anymore?
Almost no one, almost none. You fill a need for us.
We had a satellite, we had no Cosmonaut.

Control 1

"Enough science," we said. "We need imagination.
Time for the poets, the professional imaginers, to move in."
As you know we in the Soviet Union revere the poets.
Whole stadiums we fill to hear one read.

Cosmonaut

Shows how much there is to do at night.

Control 1

Poets are by nature God's best customers.
They arise from our midst in the grip of something to say.

Control 2

They are, for the most part, poverty-stricken mooches,
but from time to time one of them will incandesce.

Control 1

We thought it worth a try.

Cosmonaut

I see.

And the Soviet Union has no poets of its own?

Control 2

There were also budgetary considerations.

Control 1

And to be fair the radiation was giving us
incredible mutation problems. We needed someone
unattached—

Control 2

Or at least detachable.

Frankly, it was you or a chimpanzee.

Control 1

And no matter what you may have heard, the idea
of a monkey-at-a-typewriter was never going to fly.

Control 2

This is not some "costly but effective" scheme
for disposing of poets, such as Stalin would have approved.
This time of year the Western world is hard upon
its holidays; our people have no such false morale.
A needed boost in the battle for hegemony—
our answer to Christmas—is what this Project is about.

Control 1

Now pay attention. Your capsule has been furnished with all
the darkness that money can buy. On your right you'll see
an R.H. Wobbly word processor
with cucumber viscera and a separate drain.
To your left the slight stall of a lavatory.
These are your catchment systems.

Cosmonaut

Too many bells,
too many whistles. Paper, pen and can:
These are Ibn's cachment systems.

Control 1

We understand, you have the slight head for numbers,
and we say *Welcome* to your ineptitudes.
Our interest is in emotional findings.

Control 2

Which is why we launched you and the clean surface
of your mind. Take your telescope of fine *adroit*,
the Cassegranian Fardenarkee, the Fuji Fooey.
Turn it on the earth and tell us what you see.

Control 1

Into the little electronic frying pan
of your Dictaphone pour the ingredients of your day.
Make of your journals a collection agency.
A page a day of pungencies, that's all we ask.

Control 2

We want that poem that is the deep report.
Tell us of our planet in its heat and heart.

Control 1

Bring your particular momentum of passion to it.
Out of the unborn materials of song
sing us, if not the unsung, at least the undersung.
Give us the ethereal, the euphoria of something new.

Control 2

No doubt you will speak some number of ennobling words,
but do not use the language of a second-hand mind.
As Comrade Lenin used to say, "A sense of wonder
is prerequisite to make possible

the displacement of language into fresh response."
So speak to us in vivid and character-prone sentences.
Make us practically swoon at the effect.

COSMONAUT
Why in the good grief should I do that?
I want, only and specifically, to come home.

CONTROL 2
To this we are not in principle opposed.
When you are worn out as an instrument of passion . . .
first the report, then we talk about return.

Day 2. Wish You Were Here

Players
Ibn Opcit
Natasha Ish

A darkened stage. At center, under a spot, is our Cosmonaut. Stage right, under spot, Natasha appears.

Ish

Ibn, this is Ish. Natasha Ish.

Ibn

Natasha! I thought I'd never hear your voice again.

Ish

I finally found your frequency—and a radio
that's something more than a tin can on a string.
I'm calling from a Moscow TV station.

Ibn

And here am I, a floating voice on the single sideband.
They left me behind at the airport. What happened to you?

Ish

I still have this *job*—and you are still my *story*.

Ibn

Natasha, I was hoping I was more than that. . . .

Ish

I don't mean a "story" story. I mean . . .
you are a man in search of dignity and citizenship.
To my readers you are the citizen at the end of the world.
What happens to you matters to them—*and* to me.

So what *does* the world look like to a poet
circling the planet at 200 miles?

IBN

To live by sonic booms, by ramjet come-alongs
is not what Ibn had in mind. They send me up
to ride above the ganglia of nations,
singing "Workers of the world, ignite."
They hang me above the governments of earth to say,
"We got communism; it's better than democracy."
Well, I got news. It's all gimcrackery.
The earth was a planet before it was a globe.
A blue ball, shiny and wet, before cartographers.
It was a belle ball, corrugated green,
before borders were geometered and etched.
Ibn in his little boat looks down. From 200 miles
he sees how much God loves a rolling stone.

ISH

Can you see our host, the USSR?

IBN

Over the Soviet Onion
nothing much to see today until the fog
makes up its mind, nothing but a power plant
and its smoking connection to the sky. Say . . .
is that Chernobyl? Is that the Soviets' gift to the planet,
that smoldering pile of radiation gone wild?
Up here at the O of Soviet endeavor we see
how the logic of strap and belt have overcome
the retrograde aspects of their economy.
The merchants sell fake goods, the customers pay in bogus script
under their definition of a sound economy.
By all accounts their product is both gross and national.
By all accounts it's a poor, trashy empire.

Ish

What do you see now?

Ibn

All over Africa the sun is rising.
Glazes of ice on its physique, Kilimanyaro,
that planet pimple, fires in the kiln of the Great Rift.
Across the valley of a hundred miles
dust pillars rise like dervishes, like
suggestions from God, several at a time.
All over Africa the sun is rising
on ungovernables. Throughout Africa
a medley of burial techniques is meeting every need.

Ish

Can you see Usurpia?

Ibn

I see kingdoms
of vanished shade, places overwhelmed with what's not there.

Ish

Well, Usurpia is Usurpia no more.
The country has a new name and a new
President for Life. Nakumbo didn't last two weeks.
He saw his future poised on the tip of a spear,
and he gave a speech. But the mob was not itself that day.
First it cheered him, then it tore him limb from limb.

Ibn

And here is the lamb of North America,
to its southern mother still umbilicalled!
Over Washington we see the monumental inclines
of the builder's fathmic art—

Ish

Spillman Sponneker
has his problems, too. After dumping us
in Moscow he flew home, straight into the arms
of the back-bench bomb throwers.
Bernard E. Tacklezone has testified
on the scandal at the Food and Drugged Administration.
Senator Penfield Blowfish has made a motion,
and Senator Hudden-Huttenstutter has seconded.
The impeachment proceedings are proceeding.

Ibn

They were as famous as their sojourns will permit.
Over America Opcit learns of scope and scale.
If the Lord were to scratch a match on the Rockies, it would take
three days for that match to sizzle and quell in the Atlantic.
And where He drew his finger to complete the cross
the Mississippi filled and filed.
Above plains optically ground by glaciers,
over farmhouses noisy at night with snoring
his capsule creeps toward Phoenix, toward the flatulent
B-52s of the Arizona National Guard.
What Ibn sees is farm and forest, river and range.
Sewn fields await their summoning by rain.
Above the irregular, partial sprawl of cities at night
Ibn sees a country still in its Tocqueville surmise.

Ish

And what of home? Does Ibn see the Caribbean,
his Aegean? Has he seen his Grace?

Ibn

Among the sugar isles of the Caribée,
like casts of seed from the sower's hand,
he saw one in a surf of cursive scrolls.
Chimneys of abandoned cane plantations—
great stone awarenesses—and above those

the famed volcano, and human settlements
climbing its uneasy flanks. Ibn finds
a person's home is an enormous given.
So yes, he misses Grace. *His* Grace.

Ish

Ibn, I wish I were up there with you now.

Ibn

But I would rather be down there with you, not above
the huge earth turned below and turning but down upon it.
If we were back in prison, in that narrow bed,
I would with the simple logic of a love story
place my hand upon your clear and present thigh.

Ish

And I would turn and make of my body a home.

Ibn

Would you cover me with your nakedness?

Ish

I would, and I would with my confederate mouth
tease you into indiscretion.

Ibn

Then let my body inflate with radiance.
Let it graze your least ligatures,
tending my *needs tending* your *needs*
tending mine . . .

Ish

This isn't over. This has not begun.
I have contacts. I have a telephone.
And I'm going to get you down from there.

Day 3. The Wild Colonial Boy

Players
Opcit
Control 1
Control 2
Ish

Control 1

Good morning, Yuri Alekseyevich Gagarin Opcit.
Today we have some good news and some bad.
The Soviet Union is no more. Kaput.

Cosmonaut

What's the bad news?

Control 1

There's no money left in the budget to bring you down.

Cosmonaut

I want to speak to the docent in charge.

Control 2

Good morning, Comrade. You must have some questions,
but it's the usual medley of things gone wrong.
Frankly your return was a grace note to our program; no one
realized it would cost extras of money to bring you down.

Control 1

Doubtless you will want to do your own emoting.
Tell us what you feel.

Cosmonaut

What do I *feel*?
This much joy must be illegal. I been space-shot,
monkey-jumbled, promised Valhalla, and now you tell me

there's been a rounding error in the cookie dough?
How do I feel? If I had the Bomb on board,
you and me would be coterminous.

CONTROL 2

One's anger is given to one. The question of achievement,
Comrade, is what does one turn one's anger into?
Now you can make of this, if you like, a long,
defeatist visit to the wishing well.
But I would rather introduce you to
an idea magisterial in its simplicity.
Why not consider staying aloft indefinitely,
a living monument to Socialist Realism?

COSMONAUT

I like the "living" part.

CONTROL 2

So much better than a statue in the Kremlin:
Opcit standing there in designated bronze,
a subject of constant pigeon residue.
Every 90 minutes when you pass overhead,
a citizen will say, "Him we set our watches by.
One of the venturesome of our time, him they freeze-dried."

CONTROL 1

Columbus sailed from the yachtages of history,
so why not you?

CONTROL 2

History has room, Comrade,
for only one name (except in the case of Lewis and Clark).
So I say, "We need more lights. More cameras. And we need action."

(*Enter Natasha.*)

Ish

Ibn, it's Natasha. I finally found a way
into this infernal Cosmodrome. In fact, no one
stopped me. The security guards are gone.

Cosmonaut

Natasha, they want Ibn, an accident
parading as a choice, to ride like flotsam
this ocean of atmosphere forevermore.
Tell them it's stupid.

Ish

Isn't there
a drogue chute? Why can't he come down in America?

Control 1

Sorry, we are keeping the mistakes on Soviet soil.

Control 2

You expect us to stand here and cry for you
because you're going to die? Well, so are we
in 80 boring years or so.

Cosmonaut

Maybe this passes for humor on the chain gang,
but I sit here not sharing the shared assumptions.

Ish

Now how does he get down?

Control 2

Your job,
Comrade, is to sit in that capsule and compose.
Then to sit in that capsule and decompose.

Control 1

Comrade, don't be the ultimate offended traveler.
You're circling the earth like a wild colonial boy.

Cosmonaut

You can take *that* to a tree and tie it up.

Control 2

We sent you up there as a public service.
Don't make yourself a public nuisance.

Control 1

You weren't thinking that you would . . . filibuster this frequency.

Cosmonaut

I do have opinions. That reciprocation, for example,
is more than a principle of steam engines.
And, by the way: If I say nothing, that means "No."

(*The next morning. Control 1 and Ish remain.*)

Control 1

Control to Cosmonaut, can you hear me? Come in, come in.

Cosmonaut

The following people have a message. Please pick up the nearest white courtesy phone:

Hepatica Overruth, your issue of *Screw* magazine is ready for pick-up.
Spillman Sponneker, your limo is being towed.

Control 1

Hello, hello. Comrade, do you read me?

COSMONAUT

Corporal Nakumbo, your People will meet you
at Information. They brought a rope.

CONTROL 1

Ibn, can you hear me?

COSMONAUT

Welcome to the André Malraux Comedy Hour,
and thank you for using Tele-Sincere. How may we help you?

CONTROL 1

Good morning, Ibn Opcit. How do you hear me now?

COSMONAUT

With the forced intimacy of a pay phone in my ear.

CONTROL 1

A little volume control is good for the soul.
Our own equipment was sold for scrap today
but the Royal Observatory at Crappingstone, Whotnothit,
tells us—*3 . . . 2 . . . 1*—you're passing overhead just now.

COSMONAUT

I know, I just flushed the can.

CONTROL 1

Tomorrow
we are shutting down, we're going off the air.

ISH

Ibn, it's Natasha. How are you?

COSMONAUT

Oh, making lists
of "Things Needing to Be Done." I'm prosperous
and happy. What more revenge can there be?

Control 1

Our ECG showed you were engaged
in a privately narcotic activity last night.

Cosmonaut

Well, you didn't tell me about the contents
of the liquor locker.

Control

You mean the medicine chest?

Cosmonaut

I mean the liquor crib. Better to sleep,
I had a dram of sherry. Followed by four bottles of beer,
a tumbler of Wild Turkey neat and a jeroboam of Cabernet.
I declared a party for the human condition.
I renamed the capsule the *Gratitude Express.*
I remember giving, to inspontaneous clapping,
a lecture by radio to the faculty of Cryogenic State.
On Geo-Tamale: a theory that holds the Cosmos
to be shaped like Mexican food. Say, where's your pal?

Control 1

The Commandant? He left to take a job
as chef at *The Selective Pâté,*
now owned by the Commissar. And me,
I'm going home for Christmas. To be with my family.

Cosmonaut

This helps me understand why Christmas makes a home
for minor chords. Why Christmas is the time when sadness
can grow savage. May you find a lump of coal in your stocking.

Ish

Ibn, I've been out doing what you're doing:
Trying to sell for salvage. Scrap value is something you have.

The Germans have expressed an interest in the vessel's hulk.
But only in vacated condition. I'm sorry. It's all I have.

COSMONAUT
I will be so glad to be dead and done with all this.

ISH
Are you comfortable?

COSMONAUT
How far must the civilized
world go to find a chair with back support?

CONTROL 1
A gift from Soviet Aeroflot.

ISH
Are you warm enough?

COSMONAUT
Like a man gone overboard in an Arctic sea.
Amniotic fluid this is not.

ISH
Are you eating?

COSMONAUT
Trying to stay alive on their minimalist grist.
I'm down to some weathered noodles and a chicken stump.
I think, Natasha, we've come to the question of an epitaph.
If ever you should visit Grace, I wonder
could you, in my memory, set a union stone?
On it you might carve some fitting words.

CONTROL 1
How about *Soon to Be a Major Motion Picture?*

Ish (*To Control 1.*)
How about *You won't shut me up this easily*?

Cosmonaut
I was thinking something simple: *Olie Olie In Free.*
(Noises of turbulence and machinery.)
There is agitation here—emergency lights,
and hectic cluckings as the power fades.

Natasha, out of this mess of instruments
I have unscrewed a ring, a little metal O.
And now I place it on my finger.

Ish
A ring betokens. I'm doing the same.
There. I've done the same.

Cosmonaut
Do you feel it, this blossoming of incompletion?
The racing embrace of heart and heart?

Ish
Yours is the art of the artless.
I am honored in your heart's remark.

Ibn
I don't know if truth and beauty go together,
but honesty and beauty do. What do you do
with things that are beautiful and no longer useful?

Ish
You love them for what they are.

Cosmonaut
Love is the gentle absence of many other things.
It will be the last thing left, the final trace,
when our kind is finally done.

Control 1

I don't have a ring, you two, but I have a gift:
May you find in it a second way to wend. Ibn,
in front of you you'll find a switch named Bosnian Override.
You remember we told you it was decorative in intent,
as handy as a snow shovel in August? Well,
that is the Master Blender and Control Jammer.
To this you should fix the flywheel of your mind.
What it does is impressive and complete.

Cosmonaut

You expect me to trust this nipple of technology?

Control 1

As I see it you have two choices: You can stay
where you are until years of daunting cold make of you
an Italian ice, a parafreeze of alpenglow.
Or you can pull back on that joystick, cut the last draglines
from earth and take a sail in the solar system.

Cosmonaut

Death by frost or death by frost: I call that Hobson's Choice.
Actually I *have* been thinking to declare
my independence from the sun. I've seen
the earth and moon deep in one another's arms,
and all the planets laid out in a train,
the solar system's orrery array
of grinding, un-interfitting sprockets in search of mesh.
I think, "Time to take a portage beyond all that,
to the slightest lights of farthest stars."
Out to the scadwork of His constellations,
the gather and crab of His signature.
Out to where Opcit will hear the Creator say,
"What shall I make the speed of light today?"
Mayhap Ibn will even meet the dog star named Eternity.

Ish

Don't give up, Ibn.

Control 1

Never give up, Comrade, even if you have.
Some experiments deserve to go on forever.

Cosmonaut

You wanted Opcit's art to make a giant semblance,
to be report. But this is not to be.
Ibn's art will be to save himself.

Day 4. Ptolemy Was Right

The Cosmonaut is alone. On earth it is Christmas Eve.

Ibn

Dear "Anybody on this frequency,"
is anybody there? Into his can-on-a-string
the poet whispers, This will be my last report.
It will be like a brilliant sermon in an empty church.

When all its edicts have been disobeyed,
and the last government on earth is done,
well may the man still standing ask which one—
the government or the man—has been betrayed.
Language is a gift of God to man,
and the poet is His tool.
When all the governments on earth are done,
the man who speaks will not have been their fool.

On earth you wake and the name of the world is Christmas.
Up here Opcit at his porthole can but study
the sun like a dime-sized portion of the sky;
like a stone oven in its calm, sad roil of heat.
On earth the moonrise, like a gold dome, lights from within.
Up here the moon shows a face like a slice of chaos,
an immense killing-stone Opcit hopes like the plague to avoid.
The way to know the world is not from 200 miles.

Astronauts embark on spiritual voyages.
They fly to see meteorites directly puffing
on the moon, they land on its ulcerated face.
They pose, in the irradiated stillness, for
the Standin'-on-the-ladder, Lookin'-at-the-stars shot.
The mirrored bowls of their helmets do not show
their wide, regarding smiles. Under the whelm of the view

they become religionists. In the reduce
of gravity they jump like toxic kangaroos.
They unwrap themselves to lunar dust and they don't care.
But the way to know the world is not from 200,000 miles.

As the gravity of earth is so strong we fly to it,
so this need to engage life in some primary way.
Finally the human fascination is with each other.
This is why we mourn each other when we die.
Why finally what remains is respect, for ourselves and others.
Myself, I grow vacant before the miracle,
I grow silent before the sovereignty within.

I was ready at sunset. I was ready
in the hours when the day starts counting over.
I sit here now, in the many-layered quiet of 5 a.m.
In the tenseness preceding emancipation I put on
my shoes of wakefulness, my seven-league boots.

In the human spirit do we have a lifeless,
pockmarked asteroid, or do we have a meteor?
The answer hit me like a blessing in disguise.
I will choose the ride that only I can make.
I choose return, the deep return to earth,
to me the altogether beautiful.
Is Opcit stranded in an outer altitude? No more
than his body in its otherness circumscribes the soul.
Like the giant clam I've got only one move
but it's a good one. I will push the joystick *forward.*
In this, the acceptable year of our Lord,
I will do the Christmas override.
I will be the promise of Christmas come.

I begin to make provision for my mortality.
Oar by oar we're going to lighten ship, going
to reduce this capsule to its barest rudiments.

(*Me and the engine eye each other: That's all there is?)*
I check for emergency sufficiencies.
(Are seatbacks and tray tables returned to their upright, lost
positions?)
I listen to the capsule's signature clicks.
The on-board computer gets excited. I give it
a bunch of numbers, it gives me a bunch of numbers back.
Alpha, becka, decka, wrecka—it spits out
whole passelquods of numerology.
It declares *I got the Plan!*
I check the emotional gauges: *red line* all around.

As the tip of a plow catches the shroud of sod
and begins its work, so this pod
will homestead earth's freemantle air.
As an elevator in its infinite wisdom
shuts its doors and drops, so this capsule
in a plummet will scare the damn out of me entire.
As an oven you open to an ebullience of heat will test
the limits of temperature's ability to affect us,
so this capsule like a flame-chosen steak,
like a hamburger on a grill, will knit with heat.
Till words won't hold the weight of it this pod,
Ibn within, will break into flame like a final poem.

And it may be, on the flaxen slab of Arabia,
a shepherd will point with his crook and cry *The Star! From Bethlehem!*

And it may be, a mendicant in European woods
will look up from his mumble of misericord
and whisper *Christ! Comes the child on his ridden ray!*

And it may be a rabbi by the Red Sea's birth canal
will ask *Shapely Spirit, is it you? The one foretold?*

And it may be, all over America, children looking
for Santa sign, checking the roof for reindeer scat,
will shout *He's here! The fat man with our toys!*
It may be the capsule will come down as fully deployed
and ineffective as a shredded parachute.
Like a fire hose unheld by firemen, like a bird
with four wings, trying to fly. It may come crashing
like a load of angle iron from the sky,
like a shower of insupportable debris,
to cartwheel in a cornfield, the nose cone
70 miles away. And Opcit may come down,
all beef and brains, looking like where the sauce
hit the spaghetti. He will be dead and then some.

Or it may be he will plane as much as he plummets,
soar as much as he sinks. In a long day's journey
into Horse Sense, into Public Transportation
he will contrail the world at seven altitudes.
Descending in a flattening urgency,
executing long slow dodges to starboard, to port
he will brody the broad reaches of thunderhead,
he will thunder storm. Behind the capsule window,
the wind of Doolittle: strong enough to unsteady
a mountain, the drama of descending in snow.
At a thousand unrescued feet the Krumfpod Landing System
will deploy: Down scream the wheels, the flaps and the mud flaps.
As landing is a reach for stability in a moment
of instability, he will give the *oops*, followed by impact.
A snuff of smoke from the tires as it touches down,
and the capsule will hold the road so pretty-good,
will roll to a stop on a snowy interstate.
A *bring* as the screws unseat from the flux of the nuts,
and Opcit will emerge from his lunar cocoon.

Under an earthbound moon a farmhouse, far
afield, twinkles with lights of its own.

He begins to hum the angle-iron blues.
He begins to walk in parliamentary shoes.
In the gigantic East he can just discern
the imminence of the radiance to come.

The Play ends with the growing sound of radio static from a lost transmission.

Biographical Note

The poems of John Barr have appeared in many magazines and have been published in seven previous collections: *The War Zone* (1989), *Natural Wonders* (1991), *The Dial Painters* (1994), *Centennial Suite* (1997), all by Warwick Press; *The Hundred Fathom Curve* (1997) and *Grace* (1999), by Story Line Press; and *The Hundred Fathom Curve: New & Collected Poems* (2011) by Red Hen Press. Barr has served on the boards of the Poetry Society of America, Yaddo, and Bennington College, the latter as chairman. He has taught in the graduate writing program of Sarah Lawrence College, and was appointed in 2004 the first president of The Poetry Foundation, publisher of *Poetry* magazine. He lives in Chicago and New York. *The Adventures of Ibn Opcit* is his eighth collection.